T0065531

Prospering

Reflections by Autumn Smith

WESTBOW
PRESS®
A DIVISION OF THOMAS NELSON
& ZONDERVAN

WestBow Press books may be ordered through booksellers or by contacting:

WestBow Press
A Division of Thomas Nelson & Zondervan
1663 Liberty Drive
Bloomington, IN 47403
www.westbowpress.com
844-714-3454

ISBN: 978-1-6642-0224-5 (sc)
ISBN: 978-1-6642-0223-8 (hc)
ISBN: 978-1-6642-0373-0 (e)

Library of Congress Control Number: 2020916330

Print information available on the last page.

WestBow Press rev. date: 08/27/2020

Dedicated to:

Devin Mathes: You are my first best friend and brother. You have been leading me all of my life.

Richard Webster: I prosper in large part because of your support and encouragement. You have taught me to not worry about what other people think. If I am to succeed, I am to succeed by never compromising who I am. I am good enough.

Bill Schlatterer: You encouraged me in my darkest hours; you read my blogs and supported my writing with far more enthusiasm than I deserved. God bless you and your beautiful family.

Charles Marratt: You have made it into several pages of this book! Thank you for being my good friend and mentor. Your anecdotes have provided much memorable laughter and a bit of frustration. You are truly appreciated.

Foreword

In reflecting upon the persons who shaped my early life and beyond, I have decidedly arrived at several learned and intuitive conclusions. The individual must arrive at a point, through direct influence and most often by an innate desire to succeed, often inspired by others, to take charge of her or his life and formulate a direction and goals or at the least a firm resistance to those elements that inhibit individual growth. Opportunities vary for each individual as do life experiences. I have met many and experienced much but have met so very few that have the personal drive to overcome seemingly impossible experiences and negative influences as Autumn Smith. The discourse of her life could fill a book. What stands out is her personal faith and drive and desire to achieve not only personal self-improvement but the betterment of the life condition of all those with whom she comes in contact! Speaking personally, she has made my life a better place to live within!

—Charles Marratt, Entrepreneur

Introduction

I listen to the creaking of the deck boards as my porch swing moves gently back and forth. It sounds similar to a river in the early morning. This might seem like an odd way of describing something that on other days annoys me. Today is different. I feel myself coming alive with each sip of my coffee. I hold the warm cup in both hands and enjoy its contrast to the cool breeze that teases the comfort of my robe. I look out across my yard and smile at the freshly cut grass. I truly enjoy seeing the fruits of my weekend labor seemingly smile back at me. It's one of the rare moments when I can take a deep breath and relax.

I knew right then that I was indeed prospering in every way that mattered. Then suddenly, the swing unhinged on one side and I found myself lying bottom up with tousled robe and coffee recklessly covering me. The yard that I had admired just moments ago now mocked the mess that I had become. What did I do? What could I do? I laughed!

Life is like that. In one moment, I am on top of the world; in the next, I am humbled by the unexpected. Prosperity, to me, is the ability to laugh at chaos, learn from failure, and live fully in each moment.

Like life, this book is organized in no particular order. You will find reflections from when I worked for others in various industries randomly intermingled with more recent encounters of my life as an overwhelmed entrepreneur. You will also discover random "Smile Because . . ." tidbits throughout the book authored by me and others, and used with permission, as reminders to cherish the simple things.

I pray that through your experience with this book you will begin to embrace life as something full of humor, insight, and purpose—because sometimes prosperity looks a lot like a broken porch swing and spilled coffee.

Start Today

Eighteen degrees! The wind cut through my layers of running gear and my body begged me to stop short of my sixteen-mile commitment.

The mental compromise had begun. It was too cold. I could not run sixteen miles.

Instead, I would run one mile and then go back to the car. That would make two miles.

With two miles completed, I committed to run two more away from the car and two back, which would add a four-mile run to the two. That would make six.

With six miles complete, I felt confident that I could run three away from the car and back again, for a total of twelve.

It seemed a shame to stop now. I could run two more away and then turn back. Another four miles would make a total of sixteen!

A while later, I sat at my desk looking over my to-do list and the abundance of tasks I needed to complete. In fact, there were so many to-dos on my list that I couldn't start any of them! I was frozen. I took a deep breath and highlighted three tasks: 1) The most important; 2) The most urgent; and 3) The most time-consuming.

I immediately committed to getting the most important task accomplished. *Done.* After that, I encouraged my still-somewhat-reluctant self to get the most urgent task finished. *Done.* Next, I followed through by completing the most time-consuming task. *Done.* It seemed a shame to stop now, as I was on a roll—so I continued down the list and completed task after task.

If you think you can't run sixteen miles, run one mile. If you think you can't write a book, write one page. You just need to start somewhere, and you need to start now. You never know what you might accomplish today.

The Small Steps

I am by nature very high-strung. Nervous. Excitable. Restless. To complicate things, I am also very busy. My schedule can get overwhelming, and anyone who knows me well understands that I juggle a lot and can't always take the time I would like to for "extras." The extras are usually important to me; it's just that it's difficult for me to slow down.

So, as I'm leaving the house with my purse, my binders, my laptop, and my change of clothing, it's inevitable that I will forget something. It's nice to be able to call my assistant and say, "Can you please look on my desk and tell me what the pink sticky note on the gray folder in the top left drawer of my desk says?" I sigh in response to the evidence of my lack of focus as I humbly confirm, "Yes, the note that also has the doodle of the muffin with a mustache and glasses, that's the one."

So, it's really no surprise to anyone, especially me, when I get in my car and look at my navigation. Estimated time of arrival says 9:44 a.m. Oh no! My meeting starts at 9:45 a.m. I'll be pushing it, but never fear—Autumn Smith is here! What's surprising is that when I step out of my car after a ride of enthusiastic self-affirmation and square my shoulders to begin walking confidently into my meeting, I feel a little breeze. Yes, I did remember to put my pants on, but I failed to not only zip them up but to button them at all! *Get back in the car! Get back in the car!*

⁕⁕⁕

I was able to correct the situation with no one noticing, but I missed an entire step in a pretty universal system of preparation for daily interactions. Not a big step but, let's be honest, a really important one!

A big step was securing this particular meeting in the first place. Another big step was working with my team of professionals to develop a winning proposal. Working with my attorney to draft the contract, showing up for the conference, and delivering an amazing presentation—all big steps. But if I had walked into the room with my pants undone, none of those big things would have mattered.

We sometimes get so focused on and overwhelmed by the big steps that we take for granted how much the little steps also matter. If they are ignored, all of these things that seem insignificant can undermine the responsibilities that we perceive to be more important. In Colossians 3:23, ESV, we are taught, "Whatever you do, work heartily,, as for the Lord . . ." Big or small, it's essential to pay attention and do our best by working with all of our heart into the Lord. Consider each task a spiritual act of worship to the one who has given us abundant ability.

I once heard a Baptist minister instruct a younger pastor to stand up, speak up, shut up, and sit down. Let me rearrange this piece of advice to make it a little more relevant: Always *zip up*, *button up*, stand up, and then speak up.

The Things We Give Up

———◆◆✕◆◆———

I know that my career will make some situations difficult. Friends won't understand when I'm required to cancel plans, and partners won't appreciate my lack of availability. Yet everyone says they "understand." In fact, most people say that my ambition and focus are among the things they like about me the most.

I'm honest, so I try to tell everyone up front that my schedule is crazy. I'm on the road a lot. Things will inevitably change at the last minute. They tell me "it's okay." And it is okay, at first. But then, it's not okay. Little comments start popping up in casual conversations and sometimes things progress to the point that I feel like a failure in my personal life because of my professional success. Everyone has their insecurities. This is one of mine.

If my career is important to me, then my friends must not be. Nothing could be further from the truth. I would love to be a mom, but I can't be one biologically. I would love to not struggle with depression and anxiety, but I do. I would love to have a job that allows me to wake up in the same city more than three nights in a row every week, but I don't.

We all make sacrifices when we identify our purpose. My purpose is to help people laugh and make their lives better: more focused and more rewarding. I've waited my entire life to see how God intended to work my struggles and bad decisions into a manner that would allow me to serve others. Now that I know, it is imperative that I focus.

I know I must come across as selfish when I cancel plans or fail to make them at all. I'm not being selfish, because the truth is there is nowhere that I'd rather be than with a friend or family member. If it were up to me, I'd never miss a game or a date. I'd never reschedule a dinner.

Other people live my life in reverse. I see parents making sacrifices in their careers to raise families, and I think this is to be commended. To be perfectly honest, I am jealous. For my entire life, I foresaw myself as a wife and a mother. The day I found out that motherhood was physically not possible, it hurt—and has continued to hurt me.

It took a long time for me to find peace in recognizing that my journey is different. Not better or worse, just different. I've heard people say they'd love to do what I do. I've told others that I'd love to do what they do.

I am sometimes extremely envious of people who have "normal" lives that allow them to be home every night with the people they love. This is something I need to work and pray through. But it is what it is, and I need to believe it is this way for a reason. I need to have faith.

Faith makes sacrifice possible. What I have learned is that by accepting "what is" we are more capable of compassion. Our sacrifices enable us to love more deeply.

Never before in my life have I been able to love someone or something so much. Today, I can walk away knowing that I'm not right for this "normal" job or this relationship, even though in this moment I so badly want to be.

I am grateful that I'm able to love like this—unselfishly. Sacrificing what I want in order to let another employer find the "right" employee or to let another person find the "right" partner hurts, but sacrifice wouldn't be sacrifice if it was easy.

It is also a sacrifice that will honor the lives I change when I do what I need to do. I am humbled by every card or letter I receive that expresses appreciation for what I have done in my professional life. Every single woman, man, or child who says, "Because of you, I kept going" or "Because of your words, I launched my own business, I reconnected with a friend, I walked away from an unhealthy relationship, I set boundaries, I wrote my book, I went back to school . . ." These messages remind me that I can't stop what I'm doing. It makes my sacrifices worthwhile, although no less difficult.

Focus on making the decisions that bring honor to the people you love, the leaders you respect, and the purpose for which you have been called. It will be hard. It may even be the hardest thing you've ever done in your life.

It will take strength and maturity because one day you will have to look at someone else who is living the life you wanted. They will fill your position. They will take your place.

But if you are doing what you know to be the right thing, your life will be so fulfilling that you will feel sincere gratitude for the person who fills your absence. Most of the time, love is demonstrated in the things we give. Other times, real passion is found in everything we give up. The right folks will understand and respect both.

Old Buildings

Every morning on the way to my office, I would pass by an old gray building. To me, this two-story abandoned building was perfect. It was full of potential, and I would fantasize about owning and remodeling it. I thought about the offices I could renovate downstairs and maybe the two apartments I could own upstairs. The location was ideal and the view splendid. In my mind, I knew I'd never own this building. But in my heart, I just couldn't help believing that maybe someday I would.

Then, unexpectedly, as I was driving to work two weeks ago, my beautiful building was no longer there. I saw all the stones lying carelessly heaped in a pile as heavy equipment worked to hide the evidence that the torn-down building had ever existed at all. My heart broke.

Sometimes we build up ideals in our minds. We abandon our good sense that tells us this job isn't right. This person isn't right. This situation isn't right. Why? Because our hearts want to believe in what could be. So, what do we do when our buildings are torn down? We grieve, and that's what we need to do. We need to be able to shed a tear or an angry word when things aren't as we'd expected. The loss of hopes and dreams is every bit as painful and disappointing as losing things that really were.

What matters is what happens after we grieve. This is important, because sometimes we have a tendency to get stuck trying to pick up rubble and reconstruct buildings that were never intended for us. It's never just a building in the moment that your heart is breaking. However, you may find that after time, you drive past an empty lot and forget the building was ever there at all. Time makes this possible, so take all the time you need. With enough time, you may even find that something new and exciting is constructed where the old building once stood decaying. Sometimes an old building needs to fall to make room for something better.

The Bible teaches us to guard our hearts: "Keep thy heart with all diligence; for out of it are the issues of life."" (Proverbs 4:23 KJV) This means to not let our imaginations carry us away but to use good sense in what and who we choose to believe and trust. This means to look beyond promising exteriors and realize that maybe it really was just an old building after all.

Unstoppable

———◆◆✕◆◆———

Sometimes it feels like I'm leading a double life. When I'm on the road, my associates need to remind me to not help the bellmen carry my luggage—that it's their job. I still cringe when I hand over my bags. It goes against every single way I was raised—to let someone do what I can do for myself. Maybe that's why I tip so generously. But that only makes matters worse. The better I tip, the harder they work. The more I tip, and . . . just like that my profits decline faster than Baskin-Robbins on ice-cream Sunday. Ridiculous.

Then there's the dinners. It's hard for me to not utter at least one hundred "thank you"s when waitstaff go above and beyond. More than once, my associates have had to lean over and remind me that "it's their job" or "I think they know you appreciate it, dear." What my associates don't know is that I was once a waitress and few, if any, of them ever were. So, I say "thank you."

My car is humble. My home is humble. Why? Because I grew up humble, and I know how seeing folks with "look at me" things made me feel as a kid. I don't ever want to make anyone else feel that way. I have what I need and even my humble possessions are more than I deserve.

I guess my frustration began about a year ago and came and went in waves until I started taking an honest look at myself. I'll be thirty-four in November and am just now discovering what's most important to me. What I like. What I don't like. Whose company I prefer to keep. I am allowing myself the only opportunity I never sought before: the opportunity to learn and, more importantly, to love who I am.

When I had very little, I always wondered if people treated me well or badly because of my circumstances. As I acquired more professionally, I found myself wondering the same thing just in a mirror image. Were people treating me one way or another because I had built something great? Now I'm at a stage where I know that how people treat me is not about me at all. It's 100 percent about them. So, I'm learning to relax.

Recently, I accepted a "normal" job. I will still speak and consult because I *love* it. But I'm also learning that I also really love my "normal" job. The people I'm meeting are real and genuine; they work hard and do good work. They are kind. I'm reconnecting with the very people I started speaking to in order to encourage in the first place, and that's incredibly important to me. I love seeing how God works things together and I pray that I won't waste any of it.

I've been reminded of a few cornerstone principles over the past two months. I've been reminded that humble is good, every job is important, and a bad attitude will never make a bad situation better. I've even experienced a renewed sense of how prosperity is achieved in the first place:

If you want to be good, make up your mind to show up. If you want to be great, show up and make up your mind to work the hardest. If you want to be the best, show up, work the hardest, and make up your mind to smile about it.

We can all be unstoppable.

From a Distance

---◆◆✕◆◆---

Everyone who knows me understands that I have a soft spot for helping critters. All critters. I will stop my afternoon runs to pick up worms baking in the sun and relocate them from the hot pavement to the cool grass. I don't like to touch them, but I do.

I am however not overly fond of turtles. I had one mishap with a snapper and now I'm a little shy of them all. Nonetheless, I will stop my car and move them out of the road when it's reasonable to do so. Other times, helping animals is much more rewarding. I grew up in the country, so the opportunities were aplenty. From stray dogs to injured bunnies, I saved them all.

You can imagine how it broke my heart to see a bird flying half-heartedly, clearly injured, and being unable to get to it. As much as I wanted to help, my attempts at rescuing it were probably causing more harm than good. It was a difficult realization. I sat in my car and contemplated whether I should try again to help the bird or not. I prayed about it and I called a friend. It was hard to leave the poor bird in God's hands, but His hands are, after all, much safer than mine and a lot less scary to a helpless sparrow. I drove away. Days later, I still thought about that bird I could not help.

Sometimes our lives are like that. We can love hundreds of people. We can care very much about them. Even when it's difficult to recognize, sometimes walking away is the kindest thing we can do. Sometimes our presence is not what's best, even when it's so badly wanted. It's not that we don't care or don't love—it's that we do, so much.

Sometimes our careers or even our dreams demand that we take a step back and reevaluate our contributions. If we have built a strong brand and established a legacy, sometimes it's time to remove ourselves and let others take the lead. Maybe it's time to trust the people we have developed enough to let them shine their own light as opposed to merely reflecting our own. Maybe it's time for a different adventure.

Moving forward doesn't mean that our core changes. If we are kind, we will continue to be kind—not just to pretty creatures but to turtles and worms and even to people who don't deserve it. Kindness should always be extended freely.

If we are leaders, we will continue to lead. If we are good, we will still be good. What's important is that we look at people and situations and determine where we can be of help by being present and when we can demonstrate greater compassion by removing ourselves and trusting God to be God.

We can't save the world, and we can't make everyone happy. Life is full of hard decisions. We need to be prepared to step up and also know when to step back. Walking away is not weakness; walking away is wisdom.

"God, help us to know when and how our gifts can best be used to serve others and to honor you. If you ask us to stay, give us strength. If you ask us to move, give us courage. Comfort us in our decisions. Forgive us and help us to forgive ourselves. Amen."

Not All Kings

It happens all the time. But, as is usually the case when I find myself in questionable territory, this time it was in a drizzling rain. I was heading home after being on the road for days. I was tired, stressed, and ready to be home—in my own bed with my dog. I was lost in thoughts of my flannel sheets and new pillows when my low-gas indicator light came on.

Oh no! I should have filled up sooner. I didn't really know where I was. When I didn't need a gas station, there were thousands. Now, in need of just one, I saw no indication that there would be an opportunity to fill up for miles and miles.

I turned on my navigation system. I trust my navigation. She (yep, it's a she, and sometimes I call her Sheila) reassured me that there was a gas station nine miles away. I trust Sheila . . . until I'm eight miles from the next exit and see nothing. No lights. No life. And, definitely no gas. But who am I to doubt my navigation? Surely this equipment has some information that I'm not privy to. I trust the GPS for no other reason than it is GPS.

I took the exit as directed and turned left. *Maybe it's a mile or so down the road*, I thought to myself. But when I "arrived at my destination," there was only a vacant lot. I was terrified and realized I had wasted precious fuel in pursuit of a phantom truck stop. GPS or not, I was lost.

Thankfully, I was able to correct myself. And I did find a reasonable place to fill up—just in time.

There will be many people who you encounter in your life. There will be many doctrines, many opinions, and lots of advice. It will seem reasonable to assume that the more prestigious of these is correct. You may hear your inner voice warning you that something is not right. Listen to that voice. Don't convince yourself that someone or something is best for you just because of who or what it is.

Kings come from a lineage of prestige. They inherit their positions. Their names ensure their positions. This doesn't mean that you should follow their lead. Sometimes the best leaders, the ones we should follow, come from unexpected places. The kid who always protected her siblings growing up in foster care? You can bet she will protect you, too. The single father who worked two, sometimes three jobs to provide for his family? He will work hard for you, too. The people who made mistakes and made a comeback? They know the way to greatness.

You won't always see the best leaders in the front. In fact, you will seldom see the best leaders in the front. Why? Because the best leaders are only in front when the front is the front line of a battle. Mostly they stand behind, and alongside, their people, ready to catch, ready to motivate, and ready to carry their team when the need arises. Being royal is glamorous. Being a leader is hard work. So, learn the difference—because not all kings are leaders and not all leaders are kings.

What Happened to Your Shoes?

I grew up, well, to be honest, barefoot. During the heat of summer, we'd load up in my Granddo's '66 Impala and ride to evening church service at the Scotland Baptist Church in rural Arkansas. We would get out, already a bit closer to time than she would like, and I would look down and realize I didn't have shoes on my country feet! "Autumn, I swear sometimes you don't have sense God gave a screwdriver," Granddo would tell me. It must have been true, because I still don't quite know what that means. Back then, it meant "We're gonna go home and get your shoes, but I'm not happy!" Thankfully, the sermon and worship would calm her down and we'd laugh about the incident on the ride home after the service. This happened more than once.

My biological dad used to tease me and say, "You sure got some Arkansas feet!" I walked on gravel and other surfaces with no discomfort. It's just the way it was. The way I was.

Years later, an employer's gentle joke: "Autumn, do we not pay you enough to afford shoes?" I smile, understanding that my shoes belong on my feet and not under my desk. The corporate world is demanding.

"Dear, what happened to your shoes?" I blush as the

handsome man beside me draws attention to the fact that five minutes into the early morning church service my classy high heels have been surrendered and are lying under the pew in front of me.

As we grow, it is natural that we reflect on where we come from, where we are now, and where we intend to go. There are things in our history that need to be adjusted. I was scrappy growing up. Clearly, a bad temper needs to be restrained. The potty mouth I acquired in adolescence had to be tamed. Hurts that I held on to, bitterness . . . those things needed to be addressed.

But there are other things. Things like integrity, honesty, and strength that need to be remembered and even fought for. I learned to work hard and respect everyone as equals. As you advance in your life and career, you may see people rejecting these values and succeeding, and it can be hard to understand and even tempting to let go of some of your own convictions.

In Psalm 73, verse 3, KJV, a similar struggle is expressed: ". . . I was envious at the foolish, when I saw the prosperity of the wicked . . ." It was not until the writer sought God that he understood the wisdom of holding true to the beliefs that he was taught. ". . .Until I went into the sanctuary of God; then understood I their end."." (Psalm 73:17, KJV) The writer concludes verse 28 by not focusing on others and their decisions but on his own heart without compromising: "But it is good for me to draw near to God..."

You may not be "back home" but you should always stay true to the lessons learned "back when." This is how you honor your history and your family. Current associates and clients will appreciate your sincerity and probably even laugh when they notice your shoes lying abandoned discreetly under your desk.

Smile Because . . .

Sometimes running is uncomfortable. Sometimes it's hard to even get out the door. Be it the weather or lingering feelings from the night before, there was a time that I would give in to the comfort of my bed for another hour and go to work groggy. Not today. Today, I forced myself up and out the door. I passed an older gentleman and gave him my usual "good morning!" greeting. Traffic stopped me at the corner of the same street and, instead of waiting patiently, I altered my route and passed the gentleman a second time. This time I stopped and chatted. He said, "I have something that I'd like to give you." He pulled a small metal box out of his pocket and emptied the contents, a collection of small crosses, into his hands. He said, "I keep these to give to people, and I'd like for you to have one." I selected a very simple cross. We held hands and prayed right there on Main Street before I continued my run. What a blessing this was for me! I smiled at the kindness of a stranger. I smiled that I was able to fellowship and express my faith openly. I smiled because I knew, in that moment, that we each have the gift of being able to make someone else smile. When life is uncomfortable, we can receive and give blessings to the people around us. We don't have to be famous. We don't even have to be successful. We just have to be willing to make a difference.

Wooden Spoons

I had a dream about swallowing a wooden spoon. I almost choked on it but didn't. After I swallowed it, I tried to cough it back up. It was uncomfortable for a minute, but then I got used to it. In my dream, after having swallowed the wooden spoon, I started to have success in everything I attempted.

It was a strange dream. I don't know how I feel about dreams. But I do know that, historically, God has used them to reveal His plans. I'm not saying this is what happened with my dream, but the symbolism was not missed. I thought about the dream casually off and on for a few days. It bothered me.

Then it occurred to me: the wooden spoon is my past—my childhood. I didn't grow up with a silver spoon. We were very poor. The wooden spoon caused me a lot of problems when I first swallowed it. It almost choked me. It could have killed me. It could have made me bitter and angry and mean. I wanted to get rid of it!

But then, something happened when I came to terms with the spoon. I became successful. When I stopped struggling against the things I could not change and accepted the opportunities not intended to help me merely survive but to prosper, I began to see blessings everywhere. God blessed me indeed!

However, even in my dream, after random victories I would remember that I had swallowed the spoon and it would be uncomfortable again. Our pasts can feel that way. No matter how much success we achieve, when we think of the past, it can still hurt us. And still, we can do nothing to change it.

Our pasts can destroy us if we don't learn to acknowledge and accept them. The very things that were meant to destroy us may be the very things that inspire us and move us to our most fulfilling futures. We should all learn to live in this moment and enjoy the moment we are in, recognizing that what our pasts and the people in it may have " . . . meant for evil . . . God meant it for good . . ." (Genesis 50:20, ESV)

When we accept our pasts and stop struggling against them, we can begin to look around and see that everyone is choking on something. This is our chance to do incredible things. Incredible things like laying our phones down to have dinner with our friends and families. Incredible things like bringing coffee to coworkers. Incredible things like praying for each other, supporting each other, and loving one another.

I believe that most "why" questions will not be answered in this life. But every now and then God gives us hints as to why something has happened. Sometimes we are reminded in subtle ways—sometimes in dreams—that God has a way of turning things around. When we seek to love Him and love other people, extraordinary things can happen with wooden spoons.

Heavy Lifting

Two one-and-a-half-inch binders full of profiles and assessment forms. One wide-ruled spiral notebook. Two textbooks. One ripped Office Depot bag containing several items. One laptop. One cable spiraling and dropping out of control. One purse full of everything from a tube of lip gloss to a water bottle—the usual things. One Bible, because I had not read it in the morning as I normally do. Two phones and a fresh cup of coffee. One carried-over contract in my teeth.

I not only retrieved all of those items from my car, I also managed to place my coffee on top of my car while I closed and locked the door and then picked up my bundle of items again with the coordination of a ninja! Not only did I do this with grace, I did it in the rain!

If I looked like I had it all together, I certainly felt like a champ. Until, two steps from the car, I felt it: the unsettling, mushy feeling on the sole of my right tennis shoe. Dog poop!

My momentum destroyed, I looked down to assess the situation and started to spill the coffee. A quick maneuver to my lips and I sipped the apostate caffeine from the edge of the cup, forgetting the contract I held within my gritted teeth. Now my coffee mockingly covered the parts of the paper that the rain had not yet violated.

With a feeling of bewilderment and borderline grief, I approached the stairs to my office. Completely dropping all my items to unlock and relock the door, because it was Saturday and no one else was there, I made it to my desk in what must have resembled a tornado sweeping through an unsuspecting village.

We all carry things. We carry responsibility like binders and contracts. We carry extras like coffee and lip gloss. We all have heavy loads. At the end of the day, some make it to their end goal in one piece, some are covered in water, and sometimes we carry so much that the entire bundle gets dropped just shy of its intended destination—outside the office door.

It doesn't matter how well we think we have it together; we eventually need help. We eventually step in poop. Eventually, we need each other. And we always need the love, grace, and forgiveness of our heavenly Father.

Psalm 55:22, ESV encourages us not to carry our own load but to "Cast your burden on the Lord and he will sustain you; He will never permit the righteous to be moved." In the same way that God cares for us, He has strategically placed wonderful people in our lives to assist and for us to assist in return—when things get too heavy.

The takeaway is this: Recognize your limitations and trust the people you love enough to reach out to them. You don't have to carry the weight of the world alone.

Smile Because...

I gave some thought to what makes me smile and discovered that there are a multitude of things. Things that make me happy. Things that make me smile. Yet, the thing that I decided makes me smile the easiest is the smile from someone else. The smile from a child is impossible to not return, even if that smile happens to be mischievous! The smiles from my family or friends convey that they are happy, and that makes me happy. The smile from a stranger brings a return smile from me and warms my heart. It reminds me of the basic good in humanity. A smile makes me smile because it's contagious. So, smile!

—Cleo Mathes, Office Manager, Mother, Grandmother

Before I Speak

Before I speak, I have learned to pause. Anger has always been my vice. Arguably righteous anger, but mostly just the rash and fearful responses to unfavorable situations outside my control. It is a characteristic that I am aware of and a product of the culture in which I was raised. I like to believe that I have evolved beyond the influence of the environment that formed most of my childhood and early adulthood. The truth, however, is that as I sit on my self-constructed throne of self-righteousness, someone will inevitably order the last of the sugar-free vanilla at Starbucks and render my latte totally undesirable, and, well, you understand . . .

Someone less qualified but more attractive receives more recognition at work. You leave a dirty dish on the counter out of spite just to see how long it takes before your partner makes a move. A week later, the half-empty soda is still sitting with a questionable ring gathering defiantly around the rim. A fender bender, leaky faucet, flat tire—we all feel anger. But before we talk badly about the coworker, yell at our partner for being a slob, kick the car, or curse the faucet, let's pause.

Let's take an honest assessment and really consider if these minor irritants warrant such a great response. There are people and issues that are worth fighting for, and there are those that truly just deserve a sarcastic smile in passing. So, before I speak, I pause. I breathe. I relax, and I respond accordingly.

The Capacity to Care

---◆▸✦◂◆---

I teared up a little on my way to the dentist. I adore my dentist and his staff. They are professional and kind—the best of the best. I trust them. That's why I have no problem going all the way to my hometown to get my teeth cleaned. However, even with their expert care and "Jesus music" playing softly in the background, I get incredibly anxious about dental procedures. I just don't like them. So recently, when I cracked a tooth, I quickly scheduled an appointment nearly two hours away from my apartment to seek treatment from Dr. Hensley and his team.

I cried the whole way there, insisting that my father figure accompany me. I cried on the way home. I canceled dinner plans that evening. My tooth, of course, was going to be okay. But it was still a devastating experience despite the excellent care that I received. When folks asked how it was, I told them the truth: "Traumatic." Perhaps that is exaggerated and unreasonable, but it is my truth and I stand firmly by it.

Sometimes what we go through may not be "that bad" compared to others. But when it's our family hurting, our careers at risk, our health—our teeth—or our happiness in jeopardy, it is very real. A beautiful new friend demonstrated this to me last week. The one person in this world who owes me absolutely nothing was the one person I knew I could count on. I called her, sobbing after a brutal blow in a personal relationship. She listened and she shared herself with me. She helped me begin to heal and she has earned my absolute loyalty.

The same beautiful girl who helped me through something that was emotionally overwhelming shared the same concern yet again when she checked on me after my dentist appointment. Sure, one incident was more difficult than the other. But she showed the same concern in both moments. Her concern wasn't in direct proportion to the circumstances; it was in direct proportion to me.

When someone calls you because they have been disappointed with a professional or personal situation—or when they have a cracked tooth—don't let your concern lessen or increase based on the circumstance. Let it be always a reflection of the love you have for that person. Sure, it may seem over-the-top to offer to drive someone two hours to a dentist appointment for something simple. But it is a beautiful thing for which I am grateful.

There's nothing worse than being terrified or hurt only to have someone say, "It's not that big a deal. You'll be okay." If someone is concerned enough to confide their feelings, it is a *big* deal to them. So please be gracious. You are changing someone's life.

The point I'm making is that there are people in the world who care too much and who love too much. Let's be those people. Let's make big deals out of birthdays, holidays, and work anniversaries. Let's cry with each other. Let's laugh with each other. Let's celebrate with each other. Let's try too hard. Let's leave puns on Post-it notes for coworkers. Let's offer to drive folks to dental appointments. Let's go out of our way.

We change the world with every opportunity we are given to care for and serve others. In every moment we are perpetuating a cycle, be it one of grace or one of difficulty, so please let's teach the world to be kind.

AUTUMN SMITH

One Mississippi, Two . . .

I get on the elevator. Those who know me well know this is not as simple as it should be for a well-adjusted adult. I hit the button, give myself a mental pep talk, and hop in. I engage in a silent count, a technique that I learned as a child to manage uncomfortable situations: "One Mississippi. Two Mississippi . . ."

When the elevator door opens, I leap out only to realize that the elevator didn't stop for me. It stopped for other people waiting to load up and ride the remainder of the way to the lobby.

Now I'm faced with a decision. Do I quickly resume my place on the elevator or act cool, walk to the end of the hall, wait a few seconds, and then come back? I resume my count: "One Mississippi. Two . . ." I wait at the end of the hall. *I totally intended to do that.*

I return to the elevator to begin the process again. Done. I land safely in the lobby. I say a silent thank-you for my protection and carry on with my business.

In life we encounter a lot of uncomfortable things. Some of those are mild, like riding elevators. Others are extremely painful. I count "Mississippi"s because I know that whatever I am going through or pushing through is temporary. In fact, nearly everything around us is temporary. Everything will pass. Decisions that are overwhelming now will ultimately be made. Angry people will eventually calm down. Challenging situations will work themselves out.

It's not always easy, but we need to try and slow down, take a few deep breaths, and focus on the eternal. This is difficult when what is temporary is relentlessly demanding our attention.

The Bible teaches us at the conclusion of Ecclesiastes, "... all has been heard; Fear God and keep His commandments, for this is the duty of man." (Ecclesiastes 12:13, ESV) This is the whole duty of man. So, try to keep perspective and know that everything else is really just a matter of counting your "Mississippi"s.

Keeping the Plant Alive

I have been at my office exactly once this week. It is Friday. This is sadly typical, as most of my time is spent working out of hotel rooms or in the car between off-site client consults. I signed the lease on my space months ago and have yet to meet all of the folks in the offices near mine. In fact, just this morning I was greeted by a lady two doors from my own, whom I have never met. She was lovely and professional, and I did my best to look just as professional in my faded blue jeans and casual blue sweater. I think my efforts were lost when I felt the need to explain that I am not a slacker but rather a hardworking entrepreneur who just truly does not have time to deal with absurdities like paperwork. What came out of my mouth instead was "I only make it to the office occasionally, mainly to keep my plant alive." A quick glance in the direction of my office revealed that this too was not a high priority. Silly *glass door*! My poor plant.

I want to be able to sum up this story with a profound thought. I want to apply practical applications about time management. Today, I can't. My plant is not at its greatest, but it's hanging in there and so am I. Success is defined differently from day to day and some days the best you can hope for is to keep the poor plant alive.

Smile Because . . .

Fear often manifests itself as unfamiliarity. Smile as you do something for the first time.

Someone Like Me

"It must be easy for someone like you . . ." Her words hung heavily somewhere between humor and offense as I took them in. *Easy for someone like me*, I thought. *Who does she think she is? Who does she think I am?*

My mind races to a time when my mother would leave water in empty pickle jars outside in the sun all day so we would have warm water to clean up with that evening. I flash back to a time when I was showing a friend a house I lived in and he said, "Oh, that's not a bad house." I blushed and lowered my head when I had to correct him. "No, not that house. The shed behind it." That's where I lived.

My story isn't much different from other folks'. People have had it better. Some have had it worse. But to say that "for someone like me" it must be easy seems a bit ignorant. There is not much easy about growing up in poverty, suffering abuse, and, years later, waking up with nightmares and headaches because of it.

There isn't much "easy" about working until 10 p.m. and waking up at 5 a.m. to hustle for a dream that others don't believe in, let alone support or encourage. After all, "It's not practical." It's not easy to hang tough when you're struggling financially and people tell you to do the "easy" thing and get a "real" job.

Yet, here I stand, both proud and unbelievably humble as

she looks at me and says, "It's probably easy for someone like you." The truth is, the struggle has made me stronger. It is why I have success. It hasn't been easy, and I am so grateful that it hasn't been.

People look at me, and if they care enough to look beyond the surface of "now," they will see my struggle. They will identify with the doubts and insecurities that I still feel, and they will be inspired to keep hanging on to the right thing even when the "easy" thing is in front of them.

What it comes down to is this: taking it "easy" and settling for an average life just isn't good enough for someone like me.

Don't Be an Oyster

I t's no secret that I like food. I *really* enjoy it. But there are some things I have learned in the last week while traveling: 1) It's inappropriate to order something like sweet potato crème brûlée and french fries together. I know because my company laughed at me when I did. (Both were delicious. Sorry not sorry.); 2) Do not ask where the face may have been on an oyster before you eat it. (Although this is an admirable attempt to overcome the fear of swallowing an oyster via anatomic knowledge, it's frowned upon.); 3) Really, don't ask anything about the food. (This includes confirming that when you consume an oyster, you are basically eating a slug—also frowned upon.)

I don't dislike oysters. However, they're not my favorite food. I don't get excited about them or drive out of my way to order them. I have never once in my life been hungry and thought, *I would sure love some oysters right now.* Not once. Pizza, I have craved. A colorful salad, I have craved. Ice cream, coffee, chocolate, grapes—I have craved all of these things but never oysters.

To some people, we are oysters. We can feel it in the way they tolerate us. They may not treat us well, but they keep us around. They don't make us happy and they don't make us better. We merely satisfy a temporary need, and that seems to be good enough. So, we sit in our cold little shells, afraid to venture out into the world of true culinary brilliance. We tend to tolerate the familiar.

My point is, it's no fun to feel like an oyster. It's much more fun to feel like a pizza. If we're honest, we all enjoy feeling loved, wanted, and cared for. We all want to feel important, so find the people who celebrate your quirky combinations, make you laugh, and make you feel safe. If you have people in your life who treat you like pizza, don't take them for granted. Instead, make sure that they know they're your sweet potato crème brûlée and french fries. And always take care of each other.

Ready to Run ... Again

I felt something peculiar while I was out on my run. Someone was watching me. I picked up my pace but soon heard footsteps behind me. I looked but saw no one. Still, there was something following me, and I was scared. I looked down at the asphalt ahead of me.

Sure enough, there were two shadows. Someone *was* behind me. I ran faster. I reasoned that it was a coincidence. I tried to calm myself to no avail. I was terrified.

I changed my route, turning corners toward more populated areas. Whoever was behind me was getting closer. When my house came into view, I made a crazy-fast dash to the door. I unlocked the door, jumped inside, and slammed it behind me. I locked it and turned on my security system. Finally, I was safe.

There are a lot of things in life that scare us. Things we don't want to confront until we're ready—until we have the proper protection. Things like people chasing us during runs, things like our pasts, things like addictions to substances or relationships. Things like abuse and abandonment. Of course, we can try to outrun these things. We can lock doors, but we can't hide inside forever. Bad people and bad situations will always be lurking outside; we just need to learn how to keep ourselves safe.

It's a lot like when I went to the bookstore last week. I thought I was ready, but I wasn't. I picked up a book about how to overcome things from my past. I opened the cover and began to scan the pages. When I came upon a journal prompt asking for specifics about abuse, I closed the book and slammed it back on the shelf. I walked as quickly away from the bookstore aisle as I had run that last twenty feet to the door of my house on the day I was followed. I wasn't ready to run. I just wasn't.

I love to run, so the idea that I would never feel safe again doing so was unreasonable. I also love the folks in my hometown, so the idea that anxiety and regret would keep me away forever is also unreasonable. I pray. I pray that God will help me to forgive others and help me to forgive myself. I pray for peace. Faith is something I always need to run toward.

I've also learned to learn from others. I've been blessed to develop friendships with people who inspire me, people who keep me safe, people who love me. Sometimes a coffee break with someone I trust is exactly what I need to keep me focused. I haven't always been good at maintaining friendships, but now more than ever I realize the importance of running with a group. Running alone is dangerous.

I've changed my route. I can't handle my fears the way I did before. Avoidance is not effective. It's like replacing running with cake—except for me cake was alcohol and the icing was unhealthy relationships. In the last few years, I've invested energy and effort into running a new route with new and healthier ways of protecting myself from the ghosts that try to chase me.

I'm not running away from things. I'm just learning to adjust my pace. I'm figuring out what I like, what I don't like, what makes me feel secure, which hills I'm ready to tackle, and which races require more training. I'm taking my time and I'm being kind to myself. I'm running again, because now . . . I'm ready.

Donuts

———◆◆◆◆◆———

Donuts. When I'm at a critically low spot, those delectable delights always seem to be my go-to—my drug of choice. When my nerves are shot and dark circles surround my eyes, I readily admit defeat and head to Shipley's!

My heart broke recently when I realized that my beloved Shipley's location had closed. But I needed my fix, so I headed across town, in the rain, to another dispensary. After entering the bustling store, I waited patiently in line. Finally, when it was my turn to place my order, my spirits lifted as I asked for one, and only one, strawberry-glazed donut.

As I began to feel better, the woman behind me growled, "Did you get the last strawberry donut?" I replied meekly, "I got a strawberry donut; I don't know if it was the last one." My answer clearly unsatisfactory to her, she rolled her eyes and stormed out!

Had I not already been worn out, I would have recognized her behavior as more of a reflection on her and less on my "misconduct" of ordering the highly desirable and rare strawberry-glazed donut.

But I was exhausted. So, I went back to my car with my prized donut feeling embarrassed, confused, and a little sick to my stomach.

Here's the secret: even the strongest and most successful people you know are hurting for reasons that you can't understand. Everyone is vulnerable. Your actions and words in moments of stress and anger can quickly cause damage that you can't always repair. In the same way, your words can heal and give hope to the most discouraged of people.

Everyone has "oh donuts" kind of days—even me. But it really comes down to this: if you've ever made me laugh, know that I love you. If you've ever seen me cry, know that I trust you, and that's not something that comes easily for me. If you've done both, you've been given the opportunity to make my life unbelievably beautiful or unbelievably painful, maybe both.

We all have the capacity to influence people, those we meet for a second and those we meet for a lifetime. Your actions, and their consequences, are not just your own. They have the capacity for changing someone's entire world.

So, choose your words with love and your actions with care. And always remember, even if you occasionally get the last strawberry-glazed donut, you truly are something special in this life.

Smile Because . . .

I was given an assignment to write a paragraph about what makes me smile. I thought of her. During my darkest moments, when I have pondered the value of my life, the thought of her makes me smile. Her aura, symbolized by a giant beating heart overfilled with love, makes me smile. Her stories of encounters with clients silently suffering life's indignities, while she makes every effort to heal them, makes me smile. The image of her beautiful facial features and gleaming, pearly white teeth is embedded in my mind and makes me smile. Her bright blue eyes, shining out like beacons in the dark, make me smile. Her struggle to overcome great adversity during her childhood and her early adult life and become a successful entrepreneur makes me smile. Her compassion and empathy for all I encounter makes me smile.

—Anonymous

Jackson

---◆►×◄◆---

There it was. Just across the street from my hotel was a perfect trail that I couldn't wait to get on after unpacking! I watched other carefree runners make their way down the shiny asphalt as I pulled into my hotel that afternoon, and I couldn't believe how lucky I was to have found this gem (or gym, if you like puns).

It didn't take me long to change out of my travel clothes and lace up my tennis shoes; I was out the lobby before I knew it! The problem was that the entire area was new construction and the busy streets had yet to install lights for cars or pedestrians. So, there I stood like a kid that had just unwrapped socks on Christmas morning.

The Jackson, Mississippi, heat beat down on me as my blood pressure began to rise. Two minutes. Now three. There was no break in the traffic. I couldn't get across! I admitted defeat and began running circles around a shopping center . . . for three miles. I was really frustrated when a puppy ran out of nowhere. And then another, bouncing more than running. I instinctively got down as they both jumped on me for some attention. It was so fun! The man who owned them quickly came to apologize and thanked me for being kind to his pups. I couldn't believe I would have missed this had I been on that silly trail.

Sometimes we work and struggle for success in professions

that we were never called to be in. Sometimes we get angry when we can't get where we were never supposed to go. And sometimes we get frustrated when we force relationships that are not right for us. We look on the other side of the fence, or across the road, and think about how wonderful things will be on the other side when in truth it's just not for us.

Had I made it to the trail, I would have missed two delightful puppies that needed and wanted me as much in that moment as I needed and wanted them. Sometimes we need to take a step back and assess where we are and what God's will is for our lives. Our work should bring us value as we bring value to our teams, and our relationships should be equally balanced in regard to respect and love.

It's time for us to stop fighting traffic and run the race set before us with joy, even if that race entails letting go of what we thought we wanted and instead includes multiple laps around a shopping center. It really doesn't matter how patient you have been or how hard you have worked to get across the street if it isn't right; you will never achieve peace. However, when you are where you are supposed to be, even parking lots are full of pleasant surprises.

Moments

I had already completed one assignment, watched six lectures, covered two chapters to fulfill continuing-education requirements, taken one test, and finished all of my professional and personal obligations for the day. I had run five miles, seen all of my scheduled clients, and given the dog a bath. It was a productive day—a typical day in my life, really.

I'm very protective of my time because I have so little of it. That's why I hesitated when one of my favorite people asked me to run. I wanted to run with him, but there were a million reasons I could give not to do so. At the top of the list, I was preparing a marketing campaign that demanded a lot of my attention. I was struggling to schedule a conference in Michigan in which I had been asked to participate.

On a personal note, I was feeling particularly insecure because my last travel opportunity had rendered me a few pounds heavier than I was a month previously. All the stress I had been enduring had caused yet another acne breakout, and I reasoned that I probably couldn't keep up with him anyway.

But on the other hand, my embarrassing moments have made up a significant portion of my speaking success. So, what's the worst that could happen: another ridiculous blog? As far as time goes, this is someone I have looked up to for years; I could make the time, couldn't I? And so what, if I'm a few pounds heavier? More to love, right?

So, I did it! I walked more than ran because I was chatting nervously the entire time. I did not keep up with him *at all*, and that was okay. Overall, it was a poor performance on my part. But it didn't matter. I had a great time, and I learned a lot about one of my heroes. I may never get the opportunity again. That is also something that's okay, because for forty-five minutes I was in the company of someone who inspired me.

Don't miss the moments that may never come again. Lots of opportunities only come once. Don't be sorry for jumping in when you get the chance. Don't be embarrassed. Don't hide anything. Just trust that everything happens for a reason. No one can take away the moments that you've already had. So, whatever it is, go for it. Don't make excuses. Don't overthink. Just take the experience for what it is and look forward to whatever may come next.

Each moment could change everything . . . or could change nothing. Either way, it's yours for the taking. Enjoy it.

Heaven Knows

It seems like a few times each month I see eyes that hold me in high esteem. I stand on stages that are too high for me and I look at people looking to me for answers. Heaven knows I've been blessed. There are no words to express the appreciation for the people who appreciate me. I am loved, and I am grateful.

It is a beautiful thing to be recognized and to have the opportunity to enrich someone's life. There is nothing better than seeing someone laughing and knowing that they are happy because, for a moment, I gave them a reason to smile. No matter how fleeting, that moment means the world to me.

My happiness, my success, and my hope lie in the hearts of anyone who grants me the opportunity to speak. My struggle, my heartache, and my fear lie in the minutes after midnight when I am awake and scared to go to sleep. When the stillness forces me to think and remember. When I turn on silly Disney movies to drown out the silence rendered by another nightmare and try to fall asleep on the couch because the bed seems inadequate to support the heaviness of my regret.

Few people know about these moments. Few people get "those" texts. The late-at-night, pray-for-me-please texts. Few people see me lose my temper. Few people see me cry. People don't pay for that. They don't want that. Who would? God does. God wants those moments in my life. He wants to hear from me at midnight. He wants to be with me when I'm eating Cheerios at 2 a.m.

The prodigal-son parable has always appealed to me. Mostly because I am very much aware of my need for grace. I am the son who wanders. The son who disappoints. God is the Father who welcomes me home. It seems like the rest of the world embodies the "good" son, when they are looking at me as though I am undeserving. When they want to see me reap the rewards of my insubordination, God is excited to have me back.

When I am given the opportunity to speak, I am able to do a great job because I understand that people hurt. Happy people hurt. Successful people hurt. Everyone hurts. That is why it is so important to me, in this world where no one is exempt from pain, to be able to offer encouragement. I am grateful for every part of my life. The good times and the bad. When I am on stage and performing beautifully, it is in the hope that someone will be better because I have been worse. Someone will be wiser because I have been foolish. Someone will be encouraged because I have been disappointed.

Because God has extended His grace to me, I am able to extend that same grace to others. So, at 2 a.m., I am praying: "God, forgive me. God, thank you for your grace. God, let this help someone tomorrow."

No More Excuses

---◆▶◀◆▶◀◆---

Excuses lay a sturdy foundation for average lives. Smile with confidence. You've got this.

How to Eat an Artichoke

My friends are undeniably classier than me. Well, except for one very special friend who I have deemed my social equal by adaptive standards of accepted etiquette. I have progressively made significant strides in adapting to cultural standards of city life, but my "country" side still reappears at randomly inappropriate times.

For example, recently at an upscale restaurant where I was dining with three of my best friends (one of them being my social equal), there were two appetizers on the table. One appetizer had bacon, which I can't eat because I am a pescatarian. The other was grilled artichoke.

Where I'm from, we not only eat a variety of weird things, we grow, catch, and raise our own. But until that evening, I had never cooked, cleaned, or eaten an artichoke. In fact, I had barely given the strange thing a curious glance when I passed it in the grocery store.

Of course, all my friends dug into the bacon-covered dish while I looked with hesitation and excitement at the mysterious vegetable in front of me. I picked up a leaf and chewed it. It was sharp and impossible to swallow, but I somehow managed to do so.

I quietly leaned over to my third friend on the right and confessed, "I'm not sure I'm eating it right." He laughed and said, "You're doing fine." He is as socially awkward as me, so why I accepted his opinion, I have no idea. I chewed on.

When he finally dug into the artichoke, he began to choke! I was smiling with a "told ya so" sort of grin but said nothing. An explainable comradeship had developed through our mutual naivete regarding culinary specialties.

Eventually, my two friends across the table started working on the artichoke as well. We both stared in amazement as they ate the center of each leaf and left the outer part abandoned. So that's how it's done!

The evening would have proceeded smoothly with no evidence of our etiquette blunder until *it* fell from my sweet friend's napkin . . . a solid wad of chewed artichoke. *Are you kidding me?* We had been discovered! We all laughed. I felt strangely betrayed that I had gone through the trouble of swallowing mine!

Sometimes in life we do the wrong thing. Sometimes we think it's not obvious until it suddenly falls out of our napkin. Other times, we think no one notices because we believe we have completely swallowed the evidence.

Our past can hurt and haunt us. We do silly things and bad things. Sometimes we do those things by accident. Other times we do those things on purpose. Why or how doesn't matter. We hurt people. We often hurt ourselves, too, with sharp edges.

Swallowing the evidence can be just as painful as the embarrassment of being discovered. Trust me, trying to bear the burden of concealing mistakes hurts not just once but twice! Anyone who has ever eaten an artichoke incorrectly understands exactly what I mean.

So, be it an artichoke or sin in our lives, we must accept that we cannot erase bad decisions. We cannot conceal them or hide them from God or from others forever. For this reason, it is very important that God has given us solid and absolute expectations of our behaviors and responsibilities to Him and to other people. Because we are human, it is even more important to acknowledge the importance of living continually under His grace.

I have been unbelievably blessed to be surrounded by people who care for me and lovingly let me know when I've messed up, who lead the way by example, and accept me for all my strange ways. I have been even more blessed to know and serve a loving and forgiving God. A God who is ". . . slow to anger and abounding in steadfast love." (Psalm 145:8 ESV)

Even if I never eat an artichoke elegantly or live quite as righteously as I should, I am convinced that nothing can separate me from the love of my Father. (Romans 8:37-39) There are no other words to acknowledge my appreciation for the grace that I have received. I am truly, truly blessed.

Simple

Mr. Charles, my good friend and mentor, and I had finished off warm cups of tea on a particularly trying day in my early struggles of building my brand, when we began discussing religion. We both agreed that faith is simple and that our relationship with God is the most fundamental element of our existence. I told Mr. Charles, "As important as my business is, and it is very important, I don't think that God will ask me about my business." Mr. Charles looked at me straight in the eyes and replied, "Yes, dear heart, but God will most certainly ask you how you conducted it." Good business, like faith, should be simple. You know right from wrong. Approach competition or, rather, opportunities and resources in a way that will support the legacy you desire to leave.

Higher than I

———— ◆◆▶◀◆◆ ————

"**D**o you remember the day I quit a great job because it just didn't feel right?" I asked my friend and mentor as we walked. The day was warm, but a cool breeze made strolling down the historic path pleasant. The older gentleman laughed, "Yes, I do! You were so excited!" Now it was my turn to laugh. I wasn't excited; I was terrified!

Truth be told, I was terrified every day for two years after that, wondering and worrying. "What if I don't get a contract this month?" and "What if I don't get a contract next month?" As we continued to talk and walk, I told him all of this. "So, what happened?" he asked, already aware that I had made peace. "I was okay every day for the past two years," I replied.

For two years, I spent 730 days worrying and absolutely 0 days being homeless or hungry. The point is that worrying is natural. Just this week, I worked with my attorney to address medical identity theft. I made a huge career decision. I contemplated a move. I filed a police report because threats were made on my life! I struggled and worried. I wrestled. I made myself crazy weighing pros and cons, considering alternatives, and evaluating possible results in my head. I cussed a little and I cried a lot.

Needless to say, all of my worry left me unable to interact with my friends and family. It left me irritable and disconnected . . . and then I worried about that, too. I couldn't focus on my work or enjoy it. Of course, I also worried about that.

I was absolutely exhausted by the time I lowered my head and said, "God, I trust you with my whole heart." In that moment, I knew that I was never in control and, even though some of my issues were valid and scary, the energy I spent dwelling on them was not helpful. I received peace in surrendering my worry to my God. And, you may have guessed it: everything is still okay.

"When my heart is overwhelmed: lead me to the rock that is higher than I." Psalm 61:2, KJV

I Have a Driver!

During a recent business trip, I found myself waiting in a hotel lobby in Alabama and fuming when my driver was a few minutes late. I assumed that he had been the victim of a terrible accident. I couldn't imagine any other reason for why he would make me wait. My thoughts raced. I would soon be late for my scheduled appearance. How would I explain this to the people who had trusted me to show up on time and speak about having life organized?

At this point, I really needed to visit the little girl's room. But I just knew that as soon as I did, my driver would show up and leave without me. I picked up my phone; a quick glance at the screen showed me that he was now eighteen minutes late. I decided I could no longer hold the two cups of coffee I had consumed hours before.

This would not be a big deal, except I felt that I should explain the situation to the front-desk staff. "Please, I need to use the girl's room really, really quick," I said. "If my driver gets here, please, please, please don't let him leave without me!" Just like that, another full minute was wasted. I went more quickly than normal and returned to the lobby. Still no driver.

I began to panic that I had missed him. But the front-desk clerk assured me that I had not. I called the company to confirm. They informed me that he was on his way. As I sat there waiting, I had the opportunity to introduce myself to the hotel's general manager—who promptly booked me for an additional speaking gig!

After I sat back down, I came to the realization that this situation, like everything else in my life, had been organized by a loving God. When my driver arrived, he was a charming young gentleman. We had a blast talking the entire way to my destination. At some point during the drive, I reflected on a time in my life when I did not know how I would pay for gas to get to my job. Another time, I cried because I needed to replace a tire that I could not afford to replace.

I was ashamed to realize how silly I had been to fume when my driver was a few minutes late. *I have a driver!* How humbling it was to know that I had doubted the sovereignty of my God in this small matter, when He had used so many of these small matters to bless the bigger picture that is my life.

It is difficult to remember that even the most frustrating and, sometimes, the most painful things in our lives can work to our good. That day, I was reminded that I have a driver! Not the bright young man who showed up to escort me in a silver unmarked Lincoln, but an omnipresent God who continually leads me faithfully.

Blame Game

Blaming only hurts you. You have been well equipped to design your own demise. Abuse and poverty can and does take a toll. Being betrayed by someone you love changes everything. Especially when this betrayal happens in your formative years, it renders you afraid and angry. My grandfather was already in the grave when I was able to forgive him. I carried anger and fear and resentment like a badge of honor until I was well into adulthood.

It was familiar and it gave me a certain fire. It propelled me and yet it was destroying me slowly. Forgiveness did nothing for him. It certainly did not bring him back from the dead. What forgiveness did was not for him. It was to liberate me. It was to bring me peace. I could blame failed marriages on the abuse. I could blame bad decisions on the failed marriages. I could blame a genetic predisposition for alcoholism to my battle with the disease. I could blame the alcoholism for many bad decisions. There is always something or someone to blame. It is justified but it is not rational nor is it helpful.

When it is all said and done, *you* suffer or prosper because of the decisions that you make. Blaming someone else does nothing to hurt them. It does not damage their lives; it damages yours. I have found that the most powerful thing you can do to overcome situations that have hurt you is to move forward in spite of the pain. Move forward. Develop yourself. ". . .

be transformed by the renewal of your mind . . ." (Romans 12:2, ESV)

Read books that interest you. Learn an instrument. Learn another language. Use your energy to become a better and more well-rounded person. You lose so much by hating and blaming others, and you gain nothing. It's never *ever* too late to invest energy and resources in yourself, but there is no time worth sacrificing to dwell on the past.

I love the *Lion King* quote when one character bops the other on the head:

"What was that for?"

To which the other replies, "It does not matter. It's in the past."

"It hurt."

"Yes, the past does hurt."

The past does hurt. Oh, how the past does hurt! But it is the past, and what we can do is learn. Forgive someone today. Forgive them because you are worth the freedom that comes from extending grace to someone who does not deserve it and realizing that we have all been forgiven for something.

Why Failure Matters

There once was a girl who failed at nothing. She graduated with honors, entered the workforce with ease, married her best friend, and raised two perfect children who also graduated with honors. Her husband never left the toilet seat up and her parents never criticized her parenting style. Of course, discipline was of no discussion because her kids never threw tantrums in the middle of a church service or in a booth at the Golden Corral. Her puppy was born house-trained and her Lexus never ran out of gas. She lived happily ever after in a castle that didn't require a mortgage. The end.

Meanwhile, in the real world, I wonder for the twentieth time, *Why are my keys in the refrigerator? Does this shirt smell clean enough to wear to the gym? Will they really issue me a ticket if I'm short one quarter at the parking meter?* The answers are as follows: My keys are in the fridge because my milk has been on the counter all night, the shirt is not in fact clean but is clean enough for the gym, and, yes, the quarter is very important.

How I make it to the end of the day on most days is a mystery and a blessing. I fail many times in a day. Sometimes little fails that lead to wasting a lot of milk and paying small parking fines. Sometimes big fails that make me consider all my previous successes to be flukes. The loss of important contracts, failed professional exams, speaking engagements that I don't land. I fail. I fail, and that's okay.

As I get older, I worry less about failure. After all, what's the worst that can happen? I allow myself to go there but I don't dwell there. The truth is failure has marked me. Just this morning, I looked in the mirror and noticed a few lines, a few dark circles, and even a few scars.

I have never felt more beautiful. Perhaps it's because I appreciate the quiet dignity that was not present in my youth, or maybe I feel as though I am moving beyond the point of victimization and in a place of strength. It's hard to say, but I am pleased. Pleased with the frame that is more slender than it was in high school. Pleased with the dedication I have invested into fitness, demonstrating a discipline I lacked in earlier years. I am pleased with the laugh lines as a recently acquired skill to laugh at the days ahead, trusting myself in ways that I never have before. Trusting God more, also.

Aging has done something marvelous for me. It has taught me that failure is not final, that I can turn bad situations around, and that God truly does work all things out for my good.

So, there once was a girl born into poverty with a speech impediment. She was raised through abuse, survived unhealthy relationships, and made bad decisions. She has lost her temper, her mind, and her keys. Her hair is, to this day, never just right. She struggles with a potty mouth and a caffeine addiction. She works hard. She is kind and generous. She manages two companies, loves her friends, and will probably never house-train her dog with 100 percent confidence. She lives mostly happily ever after. The end.

Smile Because . . .

Shamelessly eating a plate full of international food at a food fair and collapsing into a self-induced food coma on the couch short of brushing your teeth . . . Sure, I've been there. Good health is a reason to be grateful, but a splurge with friends every now and then—smile! Saving for college, a home, a retirement . . . it all has its place and is important. But spending a bit more than you should on a dress that makes you feel fabulous or on a new pair of running shoes before the old ones wear out—big smile. Do something special for you today.

Thank You, God, for My Suffering

I remember driving one night after giving what I felt was the best motivational speech of my life to one of my young trainers. I was so humbled by the opportunity to talk with and encourage him. I have talked to 600 people before and never have I felt so grateful for an opportunity as I did talking with this young man.

There he sat, twenty-four years old and discouraged. "Everything has been a struggle. I thought my retail job would be easy. It's not. Now you hire me as a trainer and it's hard, too." My head was spinning with hardcore coaching that wanted to tell him to grow up and that life is hard. I couldn't, though. Why? Because he was wounded.

I hired him with high expectations. He was an enthusiastic former star college football player. Great athletic build. To be honest, I saw a lot of my younger self in his bright eyes. But now, he had watched and participated in one of my group training events and was suddenly transformed into an insecure young kid right before my astonished eyes.

He went on to tell me that "I met my dad this week and he is a man's man." I looked at this tall and muscular young man, and all I could say was, "Look at you!" He went on to tell me that he wanted to quit. He said that his dad was in a fraternity that had required him to be tested physically and mentally. He expressed his admiration for his dad. I sat quietly praying for the words to say. I gently recapped, "So, you're telling me that your dad went through hard things and you respect that, even want to be that?" He eagerly agreed: "Exactly!" So, I asked him, "Is this hard?" He replied, "Right now, yes, this is hard!" I followed through: "Then, you gotta do it. This is your initiation." He agreed and we spent more time talking; I gave what could be the greatest pep talk of my career and concluded with "Just show up Friday for the group." Friday: "Just show up Monday." Monday: "Just show up tomorrow."

The grunt work of chasing your dreams is hard. You cannot expect it to be easy. It wasn't easy for me. It wasn't easy for anyone else who has come before you. Who do you think you are that this life and your dream should be easy? It's absolutely an experience in determination, persistence, and strength. It is absolutely hard! It's also absolutely worth it. Just show up today. Show up tomorrow. Show up one more day and then one more and then one more and one more again, always doing what needs to be done.

I was so moved by this experience that as I was driving after the chat with this young man, I prayed, "Thank you, Jesus, for every heartache and for every hard time in my life." Without these experiences, I could not have been used as I was in that moment.

Genesis 50:20, ESV reads, "...you meant evil against me, but God meant it for good, to bring about that many people should be kept alive, as they are today." I heard a pastor preach a sermon she entitled "For Such a Time as This." Esther 4:14, ESV was the foundation verse of the sermon: "...And who knows whether you have not come to the kingdom for such a time as this?"

God is preparing you, so, "Count it all joy, my brothers, when you meet trials of various kinds, for you know that the testing of your faith produces steadfastness. And let steadfastness have its full effect, that you may be perfect and complete, lacking in nothing." (James 1:2-4 ESV) Be ready.

Snow Day!

———◆◆◆◆◆———

I could hear the snow or sleet falling outside my bedroom window. I closed my eyes tightly and silently prayed, "God, please let it stop." I tried to calm my racing thoughts of 6 a.m. clients that would need to be canceled. As an entrepreneur, if I don't work, I don't get paid. Inclement weather is no excuse. My mind, as it has a tendency to do, raced furiously ahead with thoughts of the tasks I would not be able to tackle until the next day.

Then, somewhere in the depths of my racing mind, God silently reminded me of the scripture in Mark 4:18-19: "And these are they which are sown among thorns; such as hear the word. And the cares of this world, and the deceitfulness of riches, and the lusts of other things entering in, choke the word, and it becometh unfruitful."

I had been working day in and day out, often seeing my first clients before 6 a.m. and my last after 7 p.m. I was becoming choked by the cares of this world and ignoring the more eternal truth that God cares for me. Even working so many hours and days without rest, I truly was not becoming more profitable. I was becoming less effective and more exhausted.

I closed my eyes again and prayed, "God help me to appreciate this extra day of rest that you are providing. Thank you for providing for all of my needs, much more than I deserve. Please allow me to focus my thoughts on you and doing *your* work. Forgive me for taking this day and trying to make it *mine*. You are the reason I have been allowed to do what I do. Help me to not become unfruitful with the beautiful gift that I have been given but instead to prosper under your direction. Amen."

This morning, I had coffee in bed while I did my Bible study. Then I enjoyed a healthy breakfast. And later, I made a Crock-Pot full of vegetarian chili that filled my apartment with an aroma that would have made my Granddo proud. Take care of yourself and appreciate the gifts you are given. Wishing all my readers a very happy snow day!

Smile Because . . .

I step outside and the cold air hits my face like a baptism. It is invigorating after the unseasonably warm day yesterday. I can't wait to put on a soft sweater and . . . fuzzy socks! I understand that not everyone enjoys fuzzy socks with the same intensity I do, but for me there's nothing better than sinking my cold tootsies into a soft pair of fuzzy socks. Find something simple to celebrate today.

Impasta

Puns are the best! Have you heard the one about noodles? "What do you call a fake noodle? An *impasta*!" That one gets me every time! I literally laughed as I typed it, although I don't know who should receive appropriate credit for its cleverness.

It's very funny . . . unless, of course, you are feeling like an impasta.

One time I was sitting in a room full of professionals, filling in for my employer, who told me to keep great notes. Everyone in the room introduced themselves, followed by titles and credentials that I would, no doubt, need to google later. By the time the room turned to face me, I felt like a bowl of ramen noodles lost in a buffet of linguine carbonara and cavatappi!

I felt like a fake, a phony, and like all those people knew I didn't belong there. But I *was* there—not because I wandered into the wrong room and decided to act cool, but because my employer trusted me enough to place me there on her behalf.

In recognition of my situation, I did what I was raised to do. I introduced myself. "I am Autumn Smith, and I am here to represent . . ." I told the unapologetic truth, to include my title, my responsibilities, and so forth.

Regardless of where you are, it's normal and valid to feel like you're in over your head at times or like you don't belong. I feel those things often. Feelings of inadequacy plague us all from time to time and that's okay. We all just get stuck every now and then.

It's important to realize and know who you really are and what you value. In John 21:21-22: "When Peter saw him, he asked, 'Lord, what about him?' Jesus answered, 'If I want him to remain until I return, what is that to you? You follow Me!'" In other words, don't worry about him, *you* follow me.

Stop looking around and trying to imitate others who are in your world. And stop judging yourself based upon their lives. What is that to you? *You* have your own ambitions, your own struggles, and your own story. And, for the record, people love ramen noodles.

The Best Thing

———◆◆◆———

Mr. Charles shared an example with me relating to one of his employees. The gentleman came to him and explained that he was in the midst of a bad day and needed to leave early. Mr. Charles saw no harm to the team by allowing this, so he sent the employee on his way. The next day, the same worker had a flat tire and requested the afternoon off. Mr. Charles, again seeing no real threat to the employee's projects, complied and sent him on his way. The next morning, the same guy called in with a flooded basement.

Mr. Charles knew that the continuation of such behavior would begin to cause delays to projects. So, what did Mr. Charles do? He allowed his employee an excused absence, wished him the best in dealing with his basement, and asked directly, "When can I expect you back to work on a consistent basis?" Then he waited for the worker's response and made clear that he would hold him to this date and time.

I had to ask my friend and mentor, "Why did you allow him another excuse?" His answer was quite convincing. "Given his mood and his willingness to fabricate emergencies, he was in no mind to work safely with the rest of the team. Even if he did the work by the book, it would not have been good work because he would not have been happy doing it."

Mr. Charles made a decision that was best for his clients, his team, and himself. Ultimately, the quality of the work performed and the safety of his team were in the best interest of his purpose. Think of others first and always do good work.

Melted Peanut Butter

Was I hungry? No, probably not. Was I bored and home alone with a loaded pantry? Yes, I was. That's how it started. An English muffin and some peanut butter.

My gluttony was justified. It was healthy, at least. But here's the thing about peanut butter when it gets warm: it melts. And here's the thing about me: I love peanut butter. So, I really loaded the muffin up with that gooey goodness!

I settled myself down on the couch, armed with only one napkin. *Gross!* A big blob landed on my lap! I panicked and quickly turned the muffin away from my lap.

Oh no! It's dripping on the couch! On the verge of an anxiety attack, I quickly turned it in the other direction. The biggest drop yet landed squarely on the edge of my Bible.

Now I had desecrated my Bible and . . . did I really just let a naughty word slip out because I messed up the Bible? Shamefully, yes, I did.

That's a lot like how sin works. ". . . each person is tempted when he is lured and enticed by his own desire. Then desire when it has conceived give birth to sin, and sin when it is fully grown brings forth death." (James 1:14-15 ESV) We are dragged away by our own evil desire.

We take something that seems innocent, justify it, believe that we have it under control with one napkin, and then watch as it spirals out of control.

A little bit of "righteous anger" lends itself to a little bit of "harmless gossip," which in turn becomes a little "white lie"— and before you know it, you're in the gutter. Okay, so this is a bit dramatic, but everyone over the age of twelve knows exactly what I'm talking about.

This is why the Bible instructs us to guard our hearts so that we may know peace. However, at this point the peanut butter is already melted. You can ask for forgiveness, and the Bible tells us: "If we confess our sins, he is faithful and just to forgive us our sins and to cleanse us from all unrighteousness." (1 John 1:9, ESV)

That doesn't mean there is no work left to be done. God forgave me for cursing and for my gluttony, but I still had to clean up my mess. Character, trust, and reputation are difficult to rebuild.

Thankfully, the evidence of what will be remembered in my home as "the great peanut butter incident" of that year left no stains on my Bible, the couch, my clothes, the carpet, the walls, the faucets, etc. Lesson learned. Peanut butter melts. But with humbleness and care, it can be cleaned up.

Smile Because . . .

Coffee. I enjoy everything about a cup of coffee. I enjoy it in the morning with a bit of vanilla and soy milk while I read my daily scripture. I enjoy it in the evening with a slice of banana bread or pie. I enjoy it while talking with friends and associates. Something about its soothing scent and my cold hands around a hot cup puts me at ease. I enjoy it on the back porch while watching the sun come up. On long travels, it is a pick-me-up. As a child, I remember waking up early and climbing in my mom's bed where she was enjoying a cup with a sugar substitute and dairy-free creamer. My dad enjoyed his coffee black. At my grandmother's restaurant, the "usuals" would gather every morning at the table to the left and enjoy their coffee until the rest of the rural Arkansas town woke up and it was time to go to work. On Mondays, I buy someone coffee. Oftentimes it's a coworker, but sometimes it's the stranger behind me in line at the drive-thru. It's a great way to start the week. So, on my list of simple things that make me smile, coffee is very near the top.

It's Okay. Really.

———◆◆✕◆●———

It is okay to prioritize your life. It is okay to say no to things and to people that detract from your purpose. Saying no is the single most empowering word that I have embraced in my adult life! It's okay not to work a double shift if you are exhausted. It's okay to turn down a dinner invitation when you really just want to crash in PJs and watch a silly sitcom. It's okay to be kind to yourself first. It's okay.

For Ourselves

Some things that come out of my mouth astonish me. I can be quite profound! Sometimes I call my brother to ask very serious theological questions. Other times, "Brother, if I, say, boiled an egg yesterday and let it sit on the counter overnight, do you think it's okay to eat?" Incidentally, we consulted a third party on that one and decided to play it safe.

Other things that come out of my mouth are so silly they make me smile. Some things are so mean that I have to rebuke myself inwardly and apologize openly. I can be so hateful! God, forgive me, please! Not to mention the occasional curse word that still escapes.

With all the nonsense and all the wisdom that crosses my lips, nothing has surprised me more than when I uttered the following four words in absolute truth: "I really don't care." I really didn't. Not about anything. What normally would have made me smile didn't. What normally would've broken my heart didn't. What normally would've made me clench my fists and tighten my jaw just didn't. I wasn't thrilled, I wasn't scared, I wasn't moved at all. I just didn't care.

The numbness felt safe because I didn't feel anything at all. It felt like a void. What had happened to me? I had experienced too much unexpected. Too much instability. Too much hurt. I had cried too much, worried too much, hurt too much. I had surrendered. I had given up and conformed.

That's what happens. We conform with broken hearts and hopeless minds to the things that hurt us. Eventually, we've been around so many people who don't care that we stop caring, too. We don't ever believe that we will become bitter. Yet, here we are becoming the very things that scare us because it is easier than holding our own. We break and, before we know it, we are "those" people. Those people who take care of themselves and walk around with walls built around them.

We protect ourselves. No one can hurt us, because we truly just don't care anymore. We create more people just like "us" by becoming just like "them." We are exhausted. We are insecure. We are crazy. We are all of these things because we've learned to look to the people around us, the titles we hold, and the possessions we acquire to define us.

These things are lost, stolen, and destroyed. Yet we let them elevate us and drop us repeatedly to the point where we are destroyed. People lie, they let you down, and if you aren't careful, you will do the same to someone else. Why? Because it is very easy for hurt people to hurt people over and over again. And everything you hate in someone else is exactly who you are at risk of becoming.

However, there is hope! You can't be responsible for other people. You can't demand and expect the people you love to be honest, respectful, faithful . . . but you can be responsible for yourself. You can be honest and faithful.

If, instead of losing ourselves in the world of temporariness, we lose ourselves in the love of God, maybe we can move beyond the realm of mortal influence and be comforted by the eternal security of a faithful Father. If we define ourselves by His eternal nature, maybe instead of bitter we can become better. Being ". . . afflicted in every way, but not curshed; perplexed, but not driven to despair; persecuted, but not forsaken; struck down, but not destroyed."" (2 Corinthians 4:8-9 ESV)

We can't escape the people who hurt us. In fact, those people are often the ones we love the most. They will look at us and put us down when we don't share their pessimism. They certainly won't understand when we get excited about, well, pretty much everything. They will try their best to make us feel less because we are in fact more.

Our worth is far greater than anything reflected in our culture. Our identity is anchored securely in the unfailing love of God. Today, we are responsible for ourselves. We can choose to worship God and to serve others. We can love too much. We can enjoy life too much. We can pray and laugh and sing too much. Today is a new day and we can be so very glad in it.

As Hard as I Try ...

I try very hard to be a good person. I also try very hard to be a good driver. It's easy to believe that I am doing just fine in my pursuit of greatness in both of these areas. In fact, yesterday I felt secure in both my navigation skills and my humanitarian abilities. But then . . .

I stopped at a red light. I patted myself on the back. That's what good drivers do at red lights. We stop. Yes, I am indeed a great driver. I wait. I am patient, which supports that I am also a very good person. But then, after two full minutes—not two seconds that feel like two minutes, but literally two full minutes—I do the unthinkable and glance down at my phone.

In this exact second, the light changes. I don't notice and the guy behind me, whom I suspect is neither a good person nor a good driver, honks aggressively. Instinctively, I wave at him and go through the light.

My reaction would have been reasonable had my wave consisted of all five fingers, but unfortunately it excluded four of them. That's right. I gave the guy a thumbs-up, except instead of my thumb it was my middle finger.

I instantly felt very ashamed. I realized quickly that I am not a great driver. In fact, I am actually quite careless. I am also not a great person. As it turns out, I am a bit irrational.

You see, as hard as I try, I am simply not perfect. I can try harder, but I will still not be perfect.

It is easy to forget sometimes that we are so dependent on God's grace. It is when I am the most confident in my own capability to function as a flawless human that I am quickly reminded of how very flawed I am.

I am impatient. I am emotional and jealous. And I am extremely insecure. The truth is, I will probably always be these things. But God's grace proves to be sufficient time and time again. For when I am weak, He is strong!

God loves and uses the mess that I am. He places people in my life who acknowledge my imperfections but cherish me for how hard I try. I am truly very blessed.

Smile Because . . .

Clean sheets. Specifically, warm flannel sheets on a winter day, make me very happy! Sometimes during the summer, I turn the air conditioner super high just so I have a reason to retreat to the security of a clean, warm bed! This must seem silly, but it makes me smile and I am thankful for the safe place where I am able to rest.

Days Like Today

---◆◆✕◆◆---

We all have days like today. Days when you feel that sickening moment as soon as you shut the door, knowing that you have locked your keys inside. Only to then realize that you can't lock the door from the outside. Deep breath. The keys are in your hand. *How long have I lived here?*

You get honked at in the Starbucks drive-thru and drop your card when they hand it back to you. After a frustrating and somewhat embarrassing scene trying to rescue your renegade card from the asphalt, you are rewarded with bliss in a cup. Finally, things are starting to look up!

You make it all the way to work (only a few minutes late). But then you have to hit your brakes to avoid hitting the car that just whipped into your parking space right in front of you. Now you've spilled your entire coffee. Thankfully you avoided getting any coffee on your car seats. Why? Because you spilled every bit into your lap!

I had a day similar to this. Okay, it was *this* day. I can't make this stuff up. As I was going home to change, I took a brief moment to speak to the caretaker of the apartment. He's an older guy who I think God made just to make my load lighter and my spirit brighter. He gave me the most solid advice I'd received in a long time. He said, "My grandma used to tell me: if it don't come out in the wash, it'll come out in the rinse."

I wondered to myself what circumstances inspired his grandmother to utter these words and how often they were spoken with wisdom and love to her grandson, who had now repeated them to me.

The Bible tells us that "Pleasant words are as an honeycomb, sweet to the soul, and health to the bones" (Proverbs 16:24 KJV) and that we should use our words for ". . . that which is good to the use of edifying, that it may minister grace unto the hearers."...." (Ephesians 4:29, KJV)

"God, help us to use your words and ours to encourage others because no one is exempt from days like today. Amen."

Birds of a Different Feather

I love birds. But not in a cool way like I know a lot about them. It's more in the less-cool way that when one smacks into my window I take it inside and pet it until it wakes up terrified and then flies around loose in my apartment.

I know a little about birds. Not enough to identify my little rescue as a certain species when I call the vet, but enough to tell him, "I don't know, it looks like it might be one of those little hoppy birds . . . the ones that hop around on the pavement at fast-food restaurants."

I apparently possess an impressive ability to habitually misjudge the seriousness of situations as they occur. For example, I call my friend to say, "I have a baby birdie!" He says, "No you don't." I reply, "Oh yes I do, and I love him."

So, when I think that my bird has taken a turn for the worse, I call my friend again. He doesn't answer. But I know that if I call him back immediately, he'll understand the severity of the situation, excuse himself from whatever corporate meeting he might be attending, and help me.

As it turns out, and as it was explained to me, my bird was not actually an emergency. That doesn't mean I didn't cry when I thought he wouldn't make it. I prayed as I left him on the balcony out of the reach of city kitties. I thanked the Lord silently when I realized that my birdie was okay. And days later, I still think about my rescue who I affectionately named Peter.

In less than thirty minutes, this little critter left an impression on me that still lingers. If this small bird is still on my mind, think of how much an impact you can have on others!

It doesn't take a long time to make a difference in someone's life; you don't have to be a big shot to change the world. God directed a widow and ravens to care for Elijah in 1 Kings! So, smile and be kind. And don't be so proud as to not allow people to be kind to you either. You won't always be the victim and you certainly won't always be the hero, but you will always be remembered by someone.

Smile Because . . .

Have you ever watched the leaves fall in autumn? I seldom do. This fall is something different. Maybe because I am older or maybe because, for the first time in my life, I have an office with windows and am fully appreciative of the beauty of this particular season. I love the way they cascade in sheets of gold onto the ground, which then seems to be crowned with their presence. I am lost in each moment as I follow one and then two through their calm descent. I now realize that having windows in my office may not be to the advantage of my employers who pay by the hour.

AUTUMN SMITH

Panic Happens

———◆◆»«◆◆———

I remember the sense of urgency as I googled "normal" jobs. One unexpected medical bill and a *your bill is now late* text from my wireless carrier had, in two seconds and like a car on black ice, spun me out of control. *I have to get a real job*, I told myself. It was time to give up my dream of working for myself and discontinue efforts on the book that you are now reading. Fear had taken control.

With uncertainty making my head pound, I stood up from my morning devotional the next day and noticed that my ears felt "funny." My vision was blurry. I was sick to my stomach and dizzy. I quickly was on the phone calling someone. "How fast can you get here?" I was having a panic attack. I calmed down eventually but only after wondering, *Did I take my vitamins twice? Can I die of a vitamin overdose?* It was very scary.

That night, I went to bed early because my stomach was so upset. I thought if I went to sleep quickly, maybe instead of throwing up I would sleep through this and wake up well. Instead, I woke up at 3 a.m. with a pounding headache; I took aspirin. The headache persisted and I took another aspirin a few hours later. I sat down later to work, reminding myself that this was getting me nowhere.

I began to edit this manuscript when I was reminded that this is part of a beautiful story that will end in success, if I stay focused and faithful! It didn't take long for my physical symptoms of anxiety to disappear and for my enthusiasm for what I do to be reignited. I canceled an interview I had arranged the day before for a "normal" job and kept moving forward. I am thankful that I recognize I have a responsibility to empower others.

I said a silent prayer, thanking God for this very experience so that I am able to write to you now with understanding and sincere appreciation for the work you are doing in discovering and pursuing your purpose. You are on your way to great things.

Fear Not!

My sweet niece just had a birthday and I can't believe how fast she is growing. As I reflect on the many ways that she has blessed our lives, I remember one incident in particular. It was during a tornado when my brother, his wife, and little Emmy took shelter.

For those of you who have never experienced a tornado, let me tell you, there's nothing like it. From the sounds to the feeling in the air before it hits, it's scary to say the least.

I asked Emmy afterward if she was scared. Her response, "No, I kept live baby during the volcano." At the time, she confused volcanoes with tornadoes, but she kept her doll safe during the storm. Even in her innocence, she understood that she had no room for her own fear when she was taking care of something or someone else.

We are all scared senseless of something. Regardless of who you are or what you are made of, you will one day sit in a doctor's office and wait for test results for yourself or someone you love that scare you.

You will one day, if you haven't already, switch jobs, move cities, lose loved ones, take a dreaded exam, or participate in an event that is terrifying. You will make choices that are not easy and experience your own storms as you watch your family and finances struggle.

These things happen all the time, yet God tells us to "Fear

not!" many times throughout the Bible. How do you fear not when big and scary things happen all around you? The Bible makes it clear. The answer is to love.

The Bible teaches that "There is no fear in love; butperfect love casteth out fear . . ." (1 John 4:18 KJV) When we recognize that everyone is scared amid storms, we can alleviate our own fears and theirs—by focusing on keeping them safe.

Too Much

There is a phenomenon in physical training known as overtraining. Athletes who push too hard without adequate rest periods experience an altered resting heart rate, insatiable thirst, extended muscle soreness, insomnia, depression, decreased performance, and more. The same thing happens when we work ourselves ragged. It is good for us to periodically separate from our work to recharge so that we are not unintentionally sacrificing the best results. Listen to your body and watch your work. When you start to notice that you are less productive or experiencing "overwork," take a few minutes or even a couple days off. Visit a park. Visit your family. Have a coffee date with a friend. Go see a movie. It would be devastating for a career that you love to become a life you dread. Keep priorities in order so that you can love and enjoy every part of your life.

Miss Fix It

Something strange happens when a lady turns a certain age. For some, this age is twenty-five. For others, it happens at the post-thirty mark. Since I am currently preparing for my ninth annual twenty-fifth birthday next month, this "something" had to happen prematurely. But, it happened. I found hair . . . on . . . my upper lip. *Wax it off!* But I was embarrassed to go to a salon. So, I sent my spouse at the time out of the house and put wax in the microwave—which then exploded!

I instinctively grabbed the wax from the microwave. *Ouch!* It was hot and burned my hands as I slung it into the sink! Now, hot wax hung recklessly all over the kitchen! With burning hands and desperation, I grabbed chaotically at paper towels. By the time my partner returned, the paper towels were stuck and shredded all over the kitchen and across my hands. Tears filled my eyes and began spilling over my red cheeks when I offered a defeated confession, "I have a mustache."

Everyone gets into messes. We all have things that we're ashamed of, and sometimes those things creep back to life at unexpected times. We have options: 1) We can be too prideful and foolish to ask for help. We can cover up our mustaches and try to fix them before anyone notices; or 2) We can go to a salon, humble ourselves, and let a professional help.

We are taught to give our cares to God. We are encouraged to allow friends and family to offer support. And yet, we lock ourselves away and try to "fix" things ourselves. We pray without faith and we exclude our families because we don't trust them to care for us. And we don't want to bother anyone. How foolish we can be, and what messes we can make!

The Bible teaches us that God is close to the humble but opposes the proud. When we take on more than we can handle because we are too proud to admit we have a situation too big, too scary, or too shameful to allow others to help, we deny our family the honor of covering us and we put ourselves in direct opposition to God.

This week, I learned this the hard way. I made a little problem into a big mess. As my mother used to say, "Autumn is doing what Autumn does best. Autumn is making a dangerous mess!" Thankfully, I have people in my life who love me despite my messes and even help me clean them up. All things considered, I am very blessed.

Keep Going

One of my running routes begins by going downhill. I wasted a lot of runs worrying about making it back up the hill. It occurred to me one day that I was spending the first seven miles of my run worrying about the last seven. All the worrying didn't change the fact that I still had to get back up that hill; it only robbed me of the joy of the downhill portion. Enjoy each moment. If worry won't change anything, why engage in it?

Make good choices and make them one at a time. One good decision will often naturally lead to others, so don't put too much pressure on yourself. It's been my experience that if you make a lot of decisions all at once, you'll give up on all of them all at once, too. Start with one healthy choice at a time. Don't take inventory of your failures as often as you reflect on what you did right. Ask yourself at the end of the day, *What did I do right today?*

You *can't* control other people. You *can* control yourself and your decisions. You can't make him or her or them happy any more than you can depend on them for your happiness. You can't control an unwanted or unexpected diagnosis. You can control your decision to wake up and make your bed, prepare a healthy breakfast, and go for a brisk walk. Don't relinquish the elements that you control because you're frustrated or discouraged by those that you cannot. Just like a good decision is followed by other good choices, bad decisions spiral. Keep your composure against the odds. Keep your head up and keep moving.

Finding Pennies

By 10 a.m. I've read my Bible, prayed for my family and friends, cleaned my apartment, started a load of laundry, completed social media–management demands for three companies, seen two clients, stopped by the office, finished one errand, literally ran three miles, and followed up with stretching. By noon I've devoted time to playing the piano, led two group training classes, and scheduled multiple meetings for the following week.

It may seem strange that, among my many professional demands, I've allotted time for playing the piano and studying the Bible. But those moments when I slow down are vital to my day's success.

I love running downtown. I love the activity of people as they come alive with the city. This morning, I even established a personal record with my run. I dodged familiar traffic and felt pleased with my pace.

My run was great, but the reward for my efforts came at the end of my workout during the cool-down walk. I looked down and saw a shiny penny, its head up on the pavement, in front of me. If I hadn't taken the time to slow down, I would have missed this reminder that "everything will be okay."

Some people believe that pennies are good luck. I've certainly never known finding money to be bad luck. I've heard people say they pick up every penny they come across because of the inscription *In God We Trust*. That's a very good reason to pick up a shiny penny indeed! I pick them up because they make me smile.

Slowing down during the day, especially at the beginning of the day as I do to devote time to Bible study and prayer, allows me to notice shiny pennies—those unique moments and blessings that we might otherwise overlook or ignore.

I devote the first part of my day to time with Jesus. I consult Him about my family, my business, and just about anything else that is on my mind. I enjoy a cup of coffee as I read His word. Although I sometimes struggle with understanding what has been written, I find peace and wisdom in His instructions. This establishes the tone for the remainder of my day.

The time I spend playing the piano midmorning, I just enjoy. I make time for that because it calms the chaos that could easily overwhelm me during each day. It's just another shiny penny that I give to myself.

This fast-paced world is fun. It's exciting and full of possibilities and responsibilities. But it's very easy to lose our focus and faith. We all need to slow down. Because when all is said and done, we want to be able to remember those special moments—finding pennies.

Smile Because . . .

At 5:45 a.m. I am asking myself, *How did I ever agree to work night shift?* By 6:15 a.m., my thoughts have developed into spoken vocalizations as I ask others, "Why do I work night shift?" At 7:05 a.m., I remember: There is nothing more energizing than watching the sun come up. Had I been working "regular" hours, I would still be inside forcing myself out of bed and rushing around trying to find my keys before frenziedly walking out the door well past the first light of the day. As it is, I am driving home after a completed work shift, feeling accomplished, and enjoying this daily phenomenon. I smile.

Don't Settle—Get What You Ask For

———◆◆◆———

"Is there anything you can't do?" Great question!
This morning, I apparently can't properly order coffee. I was heading to my first meeting and stopped at my favorite place for coffee. I always order the same thing: a venti flat white with sugar-free vanilla and soy. I ordered, but I noticed on the screen it read *venti flat white with sugar-free vanilla*. No mention of the soy.

Because I am who I am, I mentioned it. "Did you get the soy?" The barista responded with a reassuring "Yes," but, as is my nature, I was skeptical. Sure enough, when I got to the window, I was handed a venti flat white with sugar-free vanilla and regular milk. So, I handed it back.

He brought me back a venti flat white with regular vanilla and soy milk. I took a deep breath and handed it back again, this time certain that I was going to get more than just sugar-free vanilla and soy in my coffee. "Oh," he said, "you wanted sugar-free vanilla *and* soy!" *Bless his heart.*

Sometimes you don't get what you ask for, but you never get what you don't ask for. People who are successful have asked for a lot. They've worked for a lot, and they've never believed that they couldn't do what they set out to do. They sometimes got half of what they asked for and they didn't settle. My point is, don't settle. Send that coffee back! Still not what you asked for? Try again.

If your life or career isn't what you want, keep hustling. Hustle when other people slack. Work when they stop. Keep working. Keep asking. Take the *no*s and *almost*s and turn them into something beautiful. People won't always understand what you're asking for. People won't always *want* to give you what you're after, and people won't always *be able* to give you what you need. But that's okay.

Asking for something does not mean dreaming about how you want things to be. It's not asking someone to hand you anything. Instead, it's asking for opportunities. Opportunities to work hard. Opportunities to prove yourself.

I love the quote by Thomas Edison that says, "Opportunity is missed by most people because it is dressed in overalls and looks like work." You don't ask for talent; you develop it, you market it, you build your brand, and then you enjoy what you have earned.

My Granddo, with an eighth-grade education, taught me more about business than any college course I've ever taken. She loved me to my potential. She taught me how to run a business before I ever dreamed of becoming an entrepreneur. She worked on her feet from daybreak to dark to make her business successful. I knew from the minute I decided to go into business for myself that it would not be easy. I had no false illusions of simplicity. She showed me truth, and I was prepared because she prepared me.

I learned early on that if I make fifty calls and forty-nine of them are "no"s, it's not that bad. I only need one "yes." If I secure four keynote speeches when I've asked for 100, my bills are paid. Next time, I'll ask for 200 and I'll secure eight. It will be a great year. If I didn't ask at all, I'd be broke. As it is, I'll continue to make decisions when other people hesitate. I'll take risks where I can afford to take them and I'll get most of what I ask for. That's business and that's life.

Never be afraid to ask for what you're not afraid to work for. You can have success in whatever way you define it. You can have healthy relationships. You can have a fulfilling career doing what you love. You can even have sugar-free vanilla *and* soy milk in your coffee. Get what you ask for and don't settle for less.

Those People

There are those people. Those people who talk too loudly on airplanes. Those people who talk too loudly in general. Those people who put the toilet-paper roll upside down or, worse, they leave the very last square and put a new roll on top of the sink! Those people. And why do those people annoy us? Because we also have something to say, but we often lack the courage or confidence to say it. And because all of us hate changing the silly toilet-paper roll!

Then, there are those people who act out in ways that are cruel and unhealthy. Those people who will project their insecurities onto you, making their problems your problems. There are those people who can handle those people and then there are people like me. People who worry and fret and lose sleep over someone's careless and irresponsible words. People like me who know better, but can't help themselves.

People like me give "those people" power they don't deserve—the power to make me push away my coffee, turn down food, and lose sleep. So why is this so painful for people like me? Because I love those people who hurt me. Because I understand how miserable they must be to make the accusations they do. Because to say that I don't have my own insecurities would be beyond hypocritical.

However, to condemn someone unjustifiably, to harass me, and to threaten me is in no way okay. But those people have no problem acting irrationally. Meanwhile, people like me struggle between reacting and being compassionate. It's sad to see those people who are so beautiful not recognize that they are worthy of relationships that foster security and friendships that are mutually beneficial.

I am thankful that I've experienced my own pain. That's why I can look beyond those people and their actions and love them, pray for them, and forgive them. It is because of my pain that I can avoid telling those people that they are ding-dong bats and instead lovingly suggest that they get help—so they don't destroy relationships that are vital to their growth and well-being.

We will often be hurt by those people because we are human. But, today, let's reclaim the power we allowed them to possess yesterday. Let's wake up, make our beds, count our blessings, work out, and handle our business in a way that causes even our enemies to be at peace with us. (Proverbs 16:7, ESV)

Why Do I Do That?

———◆◆✕◆◆———

"Row 3." I repeat that twice out loud to myself as I walk into the store. Why? Because if I don't, I will inevitably spend three minutes walking around the parking lot after I come out with my groceries looking for my car.

I turn my car off and immediately turn it back on and off again. Why do I do that? Because I have an irrational fear that my car is not in park and will roll off a hill or into my apartment, unbeknownst to me, while I am covering up the evidence of a burnt dinner and surrendering again to my usual Cheerios. Reasonable.

Our quirks are all different, but we all have them. Some are justified. Some are silly. Sensible or not, the people who love you will appreciate the things that make you special. They will never ask why. They will understand that you simply are fearfully and wonderfully made and accept your entire package.

When your friends get out of your car and say, "Row 3, Row 3" before you can, keep those people in your life. The guy or gal who tells you that Cheerios are exactly what they were hoping to have for dinner and who will carry your burnt pasta out to the trash without mentioning it—they love you.

Not everyone has a place in your world. You'll recognize the people who have no place. They are the ones who will roll their eyes and ask, "Why do you do that?" when you talk to yourself. They will leave you feeling immature for getting so excited about simple things like finding pennies. They will not understand why you whisper to yourself "You're safe" before you fall asleep. They won't appreciate your admiration for Disney movies or your compulsion to bury your hash browns in ketchup.

So, the next time you leave wet towels on the floor or drive to McDonald's at 10 p.m. for a McFlurry, look around for the people who judge and the ones who say, "Pick me up an Oreo one and stop by my place before you go home!" (Thank you, Jeremy Matthey and Jon Boney!)

Determining who belongs in my life; that's exactly why I do that!

Smile Because . . .

Rain has always made me sad. I have even joked often about being solar-powered. I used to feel the oppression of the heaviness of the drops as they ruled out the potential for outdoor activities. I knew all too well the frustration of delayed traffic, slick shoes, muddy yards, and dark skies.

However, during a special part of my life, I started dating a photographer who changed all of that. He pointed out how the overcast skies created the best lighting to really "pop" the colors of streetlights and how the reflection on the streets was "remarkable." We spent a rainy Sunday downtown taking turns swapping the camera to take pictures of each other and important local landmarks. We had pizza at a local diner afterward and snuggled on the couch to watch a sappy movie that evening. It rained the entire day, and I loved it! Now, when rainy days come my way, I can't help but remember a very beautiful rainy Sunday and I smile a smile that only a lover's heart can understand.

Why Good People Go to Jail

———◆◆◆◆◆———

Good people wake up good. We wake up happy and optimistic. We don't fret when we realize we are out of toothpaste; we simply go to our travel bag and utilize what's in there as we make a mental note to replace both. We barely frown when we burn our eggs. And so what, if our socks don't match? We will rule the day!

We wake up good and we are still good when we are an hour early to get within three miles of our meeting. That is why we are good enough to text everyone at the office that we will get coffee.

That's what I did.

I also allowed plenty of time to get gas. I'm responsible. I don't pay at the pump, because some people are not good, and I've been warned. So, I go inside and wait patiently for my time to prepay. I return to the car to find that the pump is not working. I go to tell the clerk but must wait in line to do so. He pushes a button and assures me it's fixed. I return to my car. It isn't fixed. I return inside the store and wait behind four people, only for him to tell me the pump does not work. All of the others are occupied.

This is where good people begin to go bad. I say "thank you" but snarl in my head. Under my breath, I invent adjectives that would make men in the auto-parts business blush as I drive away. I will grab coffee and then get gas. However, as I pull out of the gas station my gas light comes on. Not the warning light that lets you know you have twenty miles left, but the one that reminds you that you will be stranded if you don't get gas immediately.

No longer even willing to entertain the thought that I am "good," I surrender and humble myself as I pull back into the same gas station only to wait not-so-patiently behind another vehicle to get gas. I pay at the pump because all of my "good" instincts have been exhausted. Clearly, I am on the verge of making some very bad choices.

With my car now running, I get to the coffeehouse only to find that the line extends well into the street. I can go to the one on the other road. *No, I can't.* It's five miles away and I will certainly be late for the same meeting that I was an hour early for just a moment ago. I order ahead at a less-desirable coffee place just minutes from the office.

When I arrive, I am the third car in line. I begin to think everything is okay until I sit there for ten minutes without moving. Just as I'm about to give up and back out of line, another car pulls in behind me. Now I am stuck. When I finally get the coffee, I realize that my car, which I purchased brand-new last year, only has two cup holders and I have four cups full of bad coffee.

I breathe a sigh of relief as I pull into my meeting with four minutes to spare and not a drop of spilled coffee. I think all is good until I walk in just in time to see my very good friend pouring a cup of regular coffee into his office cup. At which point I snarl, "If you so much as take a drink of that terrible coffee after I went through so much trouble to get you this terrible coffee, I swear I will never forgive you!" And that is why good people go to jail . . . obviously not literally.

Frustrating mornings are going to happen, especially if you're busy. Even good people are not exempt from the little things that add up to make a good person do bad things, use bad words, and snarl at people we care about. Beyond bad mornings, hurtful and overwhelming circumstances are also going to add up. We begin to question our existence as homes, careers, health, and families are being threatened.

It truly can be too much . . . for us. It seems like bad news seldom happens as isolated events. I remember my high school teacher, Mr. Robert Parent, telling me, "If bad things happen in bunches, good things certainly will too." I remind myself of his words often, as they have been confirmed repeatedly in my life throughout the years.

Scripture teaches us that ". . . the one who endures to the end will be saved." (Matthew 24:13 ESV) For this reason, let us focus on our race and our journey in a way that it cannot be said of us, "You were running well. Who hindered you . . ." (Galatians 5:7 ESV)

In conclusion: "Help us, Lord Jesus, to lean upon your strength, because ours is inadequate. Forgive us for those times we have allowed circumstances to determine our commitment to you. Help us to encourage others, as we have all had bad days, bad news, and bad attitudes. And Lord, please keep us good folks out of jail! Amen!"

Beautiful Things

There are days when it seems impossible to see beauty anywhere—like when you leave your hotel at 3:30 a.m. because you are scheduled for a meeting at 3 p.m. two states away.

You manage to wash your hair but negligently wad it on top of your head in a messy bun as you rush out, already in a bad mood. It will be hours before any coffee place en route is open.

The gas light comes on. The gas pump doesn't work. The gas station attendant is rude.

You glance at your emails while you grab an extremely disappointing lunch. You delete messages that suggest they may be less than pleasant before reading them.

You put your makeup on in the car, get flipped off, and cry a little.

It's difficult to push so hard. It's even more difficult to see beauty in these times. Sometimes you need to look for it—trusting that even when you can't see them, the beautiful things are still there.

In the same day . . .

It's the hairdresser whom I call in a panic when it's 12:30 in the afternoon. "Help! I have a meeting at 3 o'clock, and I need to look like I haven't been driving for twelve hours to get to it." No problem. "When you get back into town, come straight here."

Marce at Quapaw Cutters in Little Rock, you are the best of the best! People don't see you equipping me with last-minute, perfect curls. But that's what you do, and it's important to me. It's something beautiful in my life.

It's the patient soul who hides in a corner booth with me after a long day. It's his eyes that watch me shake as I unload my insecurities. It's his hands holding mine and the comfort of knowing that my secrets are safe, and my vulnerabilities will never render me as less in his eyes. He is extraordinarily beautiful to me.

It's the friends from whom life separates me for weeks at a time but that in the minute we are together we discover no time is lost. Our bonds are forever. It's the mini-coffee vacations in the middle of the day and the anticipation of ice-cream Sunday celebrations just around the corner that also make my life beautiful. I am very grateful.

It's the people who read my blog, knowing that my work is far more than a mere promotional campaign. It's my heart. It's my diary. When people show interest in my work, they are showing interest in me. That's something I don't deserve, and I am so blessed. Beautiful.

It's the bridges I've left intact—the maturity to be kind to people who don't deserve it, and the openhearted reception of such displays of grace that are the most beautiful. It's knowing that I'm not perfect but can still be gentle to myself anyway.

The beautiful things are not always front and center, but they are always there. We just need the courage to look for them.

Little Miss Impatient

I am probably one of the most impatient people you will ever meet. I've learned to manage this or disguise it effectively . . . sort of. I refuse to go to amusement parks because the idea of waiting in line makes me crazy. A wait of more than ten minutes at a restaurant? I'm leaving. A meeting that starts fifteen minutes late (especially when I arrive fifteen minutes early)? My ears are ringing and, wow, there are a lot of red lights in this city!

I go into restaurants with a plan. I've already assessed the menu online because my dietary needs are different than most people's. I know what I want. So, when I arrive my typical fifteen-to-twenty minutes early and wait for you to be a bit late, it *is* a problem. And unless you had a real emergency or are a cherished friend or associate, we will not be meeting again.

You can imagine my frustration when I recently sat waiting patiently for an associate at a table, already equipped to make decisions, complete the necessary discussion topics, and excuse myself. He arrived late and read every option on the menu. Then he ordered an appetizer. Then he asked the waiter about the specials—or, to be more accurate, he interrogated the waiter about the specials. And then he ordered something totally different. He chewed so slowly that my plate was empty before he finished his salad.

He then ordered wine. Not as in "can you recommend a red and surprise me?" No, that is how I order wine. He ordered it by systematically reviewing the drink menu and sampling not two but four varieties before then ordering a white zinfandel. I was elated when his plate was finally empty. But then he ordered dessert. He wanted dessert! I ordered coffee. We had been at the table for two and a half hours!

I was frustrated beyond reason and asked for the check. I paid the bill just to get out of there! I politely excused myself from an evening of wasted time.

The time was in fact wasted. Not because I sat at the table with an associate for so long, but because I sat at the table with an associate for so long thinking about other things I needed to do. I worried and fretted for almost three hours with absolutely nothing to show for it. I wasn't happier. I wasn't better for it. It made very little difference to my bottom line.

But it could have . . .

I could have enjoyed his story about his grandchildren. I could have been happier because of the time spent smiling at his antics toward life in general and possibly even enjoyed his commentary about his daughter's childhood exploration fiascoes.

I could have learned something about business by listening to his stories about his career. I could also have learned something about life by listening to his potentially engaging story of illness and recovery. I could have been a better person because of his testimony.

I could also have improved my bottom line, had I been present enough to request a renewed contract instead of rushing out in a hurry to get home.

It is in my nature to rush. I am busy, and time is scarce. But when I start feeling rushed, I need to take a deep breath and remind myself that time can only truly be wasted if I refuse to recognize the potential of each moment.

"I pray now for wisdom, both for myself and for others. I pray that no time be wasted living in another moment, be it the past which is over or be it the future which we are not promised. I pray that our experiences make us better and happier. I pray peace to all."

When You Get Time ...

Before I begin my rant, I should provide sufficient background information to really give you a sense of the severity of my frustration. First, I will acknowledge that I may be a bit impatient. However, last year I signed my business phone contract with a company that I will not mention by name. (Although, I will say that it is not Verizon, and you may use your deductive reasoning skills as you wish.)

I have had issues with this company ever since I signed the contract with them! For starters, I could not set up my online account. I spent an hour on the phone the first month only to be told that there was a "glitch" and I would need to go into the store. I did.

Once I was at the store, I spent an hour with the manager (who was wonderful) trying to fix the problem. She could not, and she became frustrated herself after calling the main office only to be placed on hold for approximately thirty minutes. Despite the amount of time I spent at the store, I had absolutely no resolution and would spend the next ten months and, I suspect, all future months with this company going into this location and paying at the kiosk in their store. No big deal. The folks are nice and it's not too far out of the way.

However, today I was unable to pay at the kiosk. Why? Because it did not recognize my number. My account seemed to have vanished. With my phone still fully functional and with a credit on my phantom account, I sought the assistance of an associate. Again, the lady who previously helped me was very kind. But after twenty minutes I was told, "When you get the time, come back in tomorrow." WHEN. I. GET. THE. TIME!

I don't *get* time. I had five minutes that turned into twenty and now when I "get" more time, I am to use it to drive across town to pay a bill that should have been paid in the five minutes allotted to the task this morning!

Just to put it into perspective, by 10 a.m., when their doors have just opened, I have seen five clients. I have reviewed and published social-media posts for four companies. I have done a Bible study. I have run three to five miles. I have reviewed at least two or three contracts. And I have answered anywhere from fifteen to twenty emails, confirmed the calendars of three different offices, and completed a CE report. And yet, this sweet girl tells me, "When. I. Get. Time . . ."

Time is funny and, if we're honest, most of our time is spent in vain. Like Ecclesiastes 1:1-8 (NIV):

> "Meaningless! Meaningless!"
> says the Teacher.
> "Utterly meaningless!
> Everything is meaningless."
> What do people gain from all their labors
> at which they toil under the sun?
> Generations come and generations go,
> but the earth remains forever.
> The sun rises and the sun sets,
> and hurries back to where it rises.
> The wind blows to the south

and turns to the north;
round and round it goes,
ever returning on its course.
All streams flow into the sea,
yet the sea is never full.
To the place the streams come from,
there they return again.
All things are wearisome . . .

And yet, we keep ourselves busy. We push on and we avoid whatever monsters our heads have convinced us are real. We work sixteen to twenty hours straight because our hearts are broken, our families are dysfunctional, and our memories shame us into a relentless pursuit of justification through achievement.

Perhaps the best thing we can do is realize that our purpose is not to make more, acquire more, and do more. Our purpose is to serve God.

"The end of the matter; all has been heard. Fear God and keep His commandments, for this is the whole duty of man." (Ecclesiastes 12:13 ESV)

We expect ourselves to carry burdens, fight battles, and overcome overwhelming circumstances that we simply cannot. We spend time trying to measure up when we all fall short.

But not today. Today, I will acknowledge my self-doubt and my insecurities along with my shame, and I will do what must be done anyway. I will not pretend that these things do not exist in my life. They do exist, and they hurt. But I will not waste time trying to live outside of my purpose and duty as a child of Christ.

If I adjust the way I spend my time to reflect my purpose, I will do exactly as Scripture teaches and love the Lord with all my heart and love my neighbor as I love myself. This means that I will cast my worries upon the Lord and trust Him to care for all of my needs. It also means that I will smile at the store associate when I go back to pay my bill, again . . . when I get time.

First Things First

———◆►✖◄◆———

I lost my purse. I put my phone down to find my purse. I found my purse. I lost my phone. Where are my keys? And so it goes . . .

I am accustomed to losing control of the day. And most days I am equally prepared to do so around 1 or 2 p.m. I am not, however, prepared for this type of chaos before 7:30 a.m. Today, I surrendered control of all daily circumstances before 6:30 a.m.

I had already missed one appointment. I had already been forced to call an associate who graciously walked me through an entire administrative process. I was asked to resubmit a proposal, and I reluctantly rescheduled a 12:30 p.m. meeting. I cried a little when my 9 a.m. appointment was late. By the time I realized I was double-booked at 10:30 a.m., all I could do was laugh like a crazy person.

With all the urgent and important things to do, what did I do? First things first, of course! Because I have had days like this before, I recognized that there were less than twenty-four hours left to endure. In my optimism to start fresh, I did the math and realized there were actually less than eleven hours to go. So, I did what any professional would do.

I called one of my very good friends to sing "Happy Birthday" to him. Although he encouraged me not to sing it again, I think I heard him laugh. I got a cup of coffee and did my Bible study. I took a few deep breaths and remembered that

I am never really in control of anything, but that all my steps are directed by my loving heavenly Father.

Now, I am back to business marking "big rocks" off my to-do list. Will everything get finished? Nope, not even a chance. Will they all be there tomorrow? Without a doubt—and they may not get finished then.

My priorities are a bit different since I've experienced so many days like this. I trust myself to be a successful professional without neglecting the first things like serving my God to whom I owe my complete loyalty. Or the first things like being a good friend, something I failed to do earlier in my life.

What I've learned is that everything else will naturally fall into its perfect place for us when we consistently put first things first.

Let the Grass Grow

"**Y**ou seem nervous. Are you okay?"

I hear this a lot and it is because "Yes, I am nervous."

I accept the adjective because it seems kinder than being called impatient. I move at a pace that is accelerated, as opposed to hurried. I make decisions efficiently, as opposed to quickly, and I talk at an excited pace, as opposed to talking too fast.

If you ask me what I do to relax, I will tell you that I'm a runner. I never "walk" to clear my head. If I visit, I visit briefly. I value time, which I find I have little of these days. I simply move at a precipitous pace or, as my Granddo would say, "She sure don't let grass grow under her feet."

That is why when God asks me to wait or to be still, I struggle. I become frustrated, and sometimes I try to make a move on my own. In short, I make a mess of things.

I have a tendency to force relationships and business decisions only to realize after the fact that I should have waited. I should have prayed.

I find that my inability to trust God more than myself puts me in some tricky spots. I then desire quick resolutions to whatever messes I've created, and then I try to fix those as fast as possible, too.

The cycle continues until I break. When I become so exhausted and so badly in need of peace that I yell at the copy machine and cry when they don't have my flavor of ice cream on ice-cream Sunday, it is then that I finally listen and hear the gentle whisper saying to me, "Be still and know that I am God." (Psalm 46:10, ESV)

I am wired to move fast. God designed me. In fact, the way He has designed me has made what I do easier in a lot of ways. I seem perfectly situated in roles that demand quick action.

Three states in three days? No problem. Deadlines? Done. But every now and then, God reminds me to slow down—to be still and wait for His direction.

Take your time. Take a deep breath. Enjoy your career, your friends, and your family. Life is worth experiencing, and the grass is always greener when you slow down to enjoy it.

Running with Endurance

---

2 6.2 miles. The marathon, for which I had trained for months, was now over and I was the proud owner of a huge finisher medal! My tired feet crossed the finish line. My coach was waiting with open arms for what I will remember as the best hug of my life.

Injuries and setbacks, hot humid weather and below-freezing rains. I had trained on days when I couldn't wait to get outside and on days when going outside was the last thing I wanted to do. Now, it was over and it was time to reflect.

I finished something I had set out to do. This is an everyday occurrence for some but not for me. I, like many others, have in many ways adapted to this life's destructive ideology of everything that feels good is good and everything that feels bad is bad.

I have left careers, relationships, and opportunities and felt good in believing that I was looking for "the right thing"—when I was really looking for the easy thing.

We want success to come without conflict, entertainment to be readily available, and we are sure that we deserve to be happy and recognized every minute of our lives.

The minute we get uncomfortable, we justify giving up and quitting—all while blaming conditions or others for our failures.

In words, we worship God and serve others as good stewards of God's grace. But in actions, we are worshiping the god of self and serving our flesh.

The truth is, we must learn to embrace things that are not comfortable in order that we may ". . . run with endurance the race that is set before us . . ." (Hebrews 12:1, ESV)

I don't want to sacrifice the hard work that goes into building an honest career. I am no longer content to walk away from relationships and forgo the peace that complements celebrating milestone anniversaries.

I will train in a way that every race I run, I trust my coach's arms to be waiting for me. And I will worship in such a way that God will one day look at me as I cross the finish line and say: "...Well done, good and faithful servant . . ." (Matthew 25:23, ESV)

Huge medals and crowns of righteousness come through perseverance and hard work—like running with endurance. There really is no other way.

Smile Because . . .

I frequently run the same path, and I have watched a young girl training her puppy. I always compliment her as I pass by on her "fine-looking pup." She always glows. Of course, the "fine-looking pup" is a lovable mutt. A few weeks ago, as I was traveling the familiar path, I saw the young girl struggling to carry her quickly grown dog across her yard. I realized that with enough love a regular mutt can in fact transform into a very fine-looking pet! Love can do that with situations and people, too. The ordinary can quickly grow into something beautiful.

Always a Texan

There's always a Texan.

"Come to Texas with me," I ask my brother, who has remained loyal to the hills of Arkansas where we grew up. This plea is always matched with a sarcastic response that hides a little sincerity. "I can't. I don't have a passport." Fine, then. I smile.

Even better was the time I started dating an older man. "Sister, are you trying to ask me if it's okay? Ain't nothing wrong with it. You're both grown." I say, "Well, yes, brother, because I really like him. I went to visit him yesterday in Texas." His response: "Wait a minute, are you telling me he's from Texas? Sister, I'm gonna need a little bit of time to process this. Let me call you back." And . . . he hung up.

Like it or not, there's always a Texan. My Arkansas associates roll their eyes every time I sign up a new contract down south and my fans let me know that posting videos of my first football game on social media, which happened to be a Longhorns' victory, was not acceptable. And yet, there is always a Texan. Like it or not.

In fact, there are always going to be people whom we don't agree with. Things we don't like. Situations that hurt us. But when it comes down to the truth of the matter, we still must be kind. Recently, my good friend complained honestly, "I just don't like the new guy! He doesn't even try. He's lazy and not very bright." Fair enough. "Can you change him?" No. "Can you beat him up?" Obviously, no. "Will retaliating with angry words make the situation better?" Probably not. "Then why not be nice?" Seems like that is the only reasonable thing within your power to do.

I have been guilty of feeling sorry for myself when people have done me wrong or treated me unfairly. But after a marathon of Disney movies and hours of self-pity, there is never a resolution. I can't make people be kind or loyal, but I can be loyal and I can be honest and I can be kind. How I treat and respond to others is within my scope of control and is certainly my responsibility.

To put it simply, you will always be faced with situations or people whom you don't agree with for whatever reason, but don't be rude. Some things will never change but you may be surprised how glad you are to realize that . . . there is always a challenge. Always an opportunity to behave better. There is always a Texan.

When We Work in Circles

I drive around the block—not a single parking space. I do the same again. Still no parking space. I am momentarily tempted to park illegally. I'll only be a minute. No. I drive around again. Still no parking space. I refuse to park two blocks away. I have already done a pretty impressive run today and by now am rocking some wonderful black heels. I circle again. After spending so much time, I finally find a nice space.

By my third circle, onlookers must have thought I was crazy. They would have been partially correct. Clearly I have issues. By circle three, I was tempted to park illegally. Clearly that would not have ended well. By circle four, I began to think I should give up. But that fifth circle . . . that was the ticket! What if I had stopped after the first circle? Or the fourth? I would have lost a great space and ruined a great pair of new shoes.

Sometimes when you're chasing a dream, it will feel like driving in circles. It won't take long before people are looking at you like you're crazy and, before you know it, you're discouraged and ready to give up. You may also look at people succeeding in dishonest ways and consider doing it "the easy way." Don't. By giving up or by acting unethically, you will compromise something important to you, be it your integrity, your freedom, your dream, or your shoes.

Don't give up. You might not find what you're looking for

right away. Just as you won't get fit with one trip to the gym, you won't experience success in any arena of your life without doing the right thing over and over and over again. Trust me, those circles lead to great places.

What We Do Instead

———◆◆✕◆◆———

There are always a million things to be done in a day. And I am one of those people who get them done. There is no wasted time. As a child, I never remember having to be told to do my homework before I could go out and play. I didn't *want* to go out and play until the work was done. I'm just wired that way. It's possibly a genetic predisposition passed down through my Granddo—an inability to relax.

Granddo would work all day and not rest until she'd come home, made dinner, and cleaned the kitchen. Now, as an adult, I have tried to take "vacations." I have been told that I am horrible at this. Why? Because my idea of relaxation is running earlier in the day, when other people want to sleep in. Why? Because I find comfort in completing tasks in my free time that otherwise get ignored during my regular routine. Why? Because I find peace in being productive. Wasted time is silly to me.

But every now and then, I get overwhelmed. I look at the invoices I've yet to send out, the summaries yet to be submitted for review, the manuscript my publicist has been expecting for months, and I become strangely fascinated with a Jiffy greenhouse instead. I plant vegetables. Yes. When I should be scheduling appointments, following up with clients, organizing financial analyses . . . I plant vegetables.

I'm not particularly good at this. In fact, I am horrible at it! I'm also not very good at cooking, but when I find myself overcome with deadlines and outside pressures, I turn into a regular Martha Stewart. I cook. I clean. I rearrange the furniture in my house and then put it all back again. I am not by nature a procrastinator, but even I, in all my superhuman determination, am not exempt from becoming overwhelmed.

What we do is important. It has its role and that's why we work so hard to get those things done every day. But what we do instead also matters and can tell us a lot about who we are and what we value. It's okay to step away from things to clear your head—if what you do instead gives you peace and helps you feel refreshed and refocused.

Take an inventory of where your attentions turn when they turn away from the "big rocks" on your to-do list. If you find yourself overeating, drinking, or binge-watching TV, it might be time to do something else instead.

What we do instead is important, too.

Those Who Notice

———◆◆✦◆◆———

"**D**id you do something different to your hair?" *Thank you!* As a matter of fact, I did! It feels good to be noticed.

I love standing on stage and making people laugh. I love knowing that someone will go back to work or home feeling centered and refocused after one of my seminars. It goes without saying that when you are in the front of the room, people will notice. When you do something great, people notice. When people notice the less obvious, that's when it really makes a difference . . . like when you get your hair trimmed.

There are a million ways that people can tell us they care. People all do things a little differently. What is important is that we recognize when people try . . . when they notice. Not everyone will make a grand gesture. Some people will ask you how your day was. Some people will make sure that you're wearing extra layers when it's cold outside.

"Did you eat?"

"Let's grab lunch."

"Did you do something different to your hair?"

Hang on to those people. They may not always show affection the way you expect them to, but their effort is extremely rare and attractive.

Pay attention to the friends who tell you "good morning" and the ones who get up early to meet for coffee because it fits into *your* schedule. And if they give you casual hugs and make fun of your truck . . . it's probably because they don't know how to tell you that they think you're amazing . . . or you drive a Ford.

Be someone who notices. Look after your friends and never take for granted someone who is trying. In short, notice those who notice because they are forever folks.

Something Like Magic

When I'm on the road, it always amazes me that I can leave my room and when I return it's like a brand-new room. When I first started traveling, I would make my bed the way I was always taught. You get up, you make your bed. That's what happens. However, one time I didn't make my bed in a hotel room and I returned to find it was made anyway! This might sound silly to someone who has grown up much differently than how I did, but for me . . . wow!

And it's not just the beds in hotels! It's also the coffee packages that reappear and the soap and the towels! Magic! Pure magic! Then one day, I stayed in the hotel and worked. Mystery solved. Very professional people were coming in while I was out and doing all of these wonderful things to make me comfortable on my return. Unbelievable.

And then it occurred to me: I do the dishes at my house. I also do the laundry. I sometimes feel like a maid. In business, I sometimes feel like a minion. But now, I understand—I am neither a minion nor a maid . . . I am magic!

The beautiful truth is that we are all magic. All of those little things that aren't being acknowledged by your peers, your family, your employers, or anyone else are, in fact, being noticed. And while it's nice to hear verbal confirmation of a job well done, we won't always get that. Sure, it's discouraging. Sure, it's frustrating. But sometimes we have to be content to know that we are magic. It's inspiring to know that what we do matters.

Our children may never know how their homework got into their backpacks the next morning, our partners may never understand how their dirty laundry cleaned itself and reappeared in the closet. And, you know what? That's okay. It's okay to let magic be magic—and you, darling, are certainly magical.

Ghosts

I walked out into the garage and raised the garage door. It was already dark, and the rain had not let up. It was the perfect, spooky October night. I opened the back door of my car and placed my travel bags into the backseat. Then, I heard the sound of metal dragging across the asphalt of my driveway. I absolutely did not want to look up and see what was responsible for the eerie sound. But I looked anyway.

Sure enough, like a scene from a horror movie, I observed the last bit of a large chain being dragged directly in front of my open garage, within two feet of the back of my car. I learned something about myself that night. I learned that although I would like to believe that I am a ninja, I am in fact not. I froze. I also learned that no matter how much I try to hide from my ghosts, I will ultimately have to face them. I also learned that my ghosts are probably much worse in my mind than they are in real life.

My ghost on that evening turned out to be the neighbor's husky who had broken his chain. He came in search of treats that I had given him when he "visited" before. I walked him back to the neighbor's home feeling significant relief.

Ghosts come in many forms and sometimes we feed them. We may think that we are investing time and energy into hobbies or careers, when we are actually practicing avoidance. Some things are unbelievably painful, but when we continually neglect to face them we allow them to grow. Then, those ghosts turn up when weather conditions are miserable—dragging their chains with them!

We may never be able to eradicate the ghosts in our pasts. It's not fair and it's not easy. It is, however, our responsibility to deal with them. I loved on the neighbor's dog that night. I wasn't happy that he had scared me, but I came to terms with the fact that he was there. And he was not at all the monster I had created in my mind.

Sometimes depression and anxiety don't look the way we expect. Sometimes depression wears a pretty face and a smile. Anxiety doesn't always look like doing nothing; sometimes it looks like working too much, talking too much, and thinking too much. It looks a lot like a chain being pulled across a driveway.

When faced with out ghosts, we can fight, we can flee, or we can freeze. It's important to arm ourselves with what we need for battle because our grief, our guilt, and our fear will find us when we least expect it. The Bible teaches us to "Put on the whole armor of God . . ." (Ephesians 6:11 ESV) By trusting in God, we can find comfort and peace. We can claim strength through the name of Jesus. We can recognize that we *all* are running from or fighting with ghosts. We are all in battle.

Let us seek to encourage each other, pray for each other, and love each other. Let's not be a part of the chain, but instead let us be the happy, adventurous puppy at the end of it. Let's live our lives so that when others are faced with their ghosts, they are relieved to see us.

Final Thoughts

I sit pondering life: what it is, what it has been, what it will be. I see myself in the eyes of the people I have known, and man, I have known the best! I would like to say times haven't changed me, but thankfully and regrettably I am the product of those experiences. For all the "my faults," "their faults," and "society's faults," I have somehow reemerged someone stronger, someone kinder, someone I can finally live with.

Thank you for reading my reflections. Thank you for struggling with me, laughing with me, living with me through these pages of what in essence comprise my diary. If my life can't be shared with others, then what's the point? Lives are made to be shared.

Embrace your quirks and all of the things that make you uniquely you, because you are something wonderful. This world needs everything that you bring to the table. My prayer is that you love yourself, that you forgive yourself, and that you speak kindly to yourself. I pray prosperity for you, for your family, for your career, and for your community. Life can be painful, but it can also be extraordinarily beautiful. Look for the beauty and be always blessed.

With all my love,
Autumn Smith

Printed in the United States
By Bookmasters